C000274795
COBBOLD ST
Factory
THE PLAIN
FOUNDRY ROAD
Silk Factory
ORCHARD ST
PROPOSED RD
ST HELENS STREET
St Helens
County Court
County Gaol
Borough Gaol
BARCLAY ST
UPPER ORWELL ST
ORWELL PL.
ERNEST ST
VICTORIA STREET
BACK ST
BOROUGH ROAD
PRINCES ST
ALFRED ST
ARTHUR ST
POTTERY ST
MOUNT ST
HILL ST
School
Water Works
CHURCH ST
St Clement
NEW ST
St Helen's Pottery
FORE STREET
Foundation
OLD SHIRE HALL YD
LOWER
ST CLEMENTS
CHURCH ST
Custom Ho
QUAY ST
COMMON QUAY
WYKES
Trinity Ch
ALBION
THE
Factory
RANSOM
SHIP YARD
ORWELL
IRON WORKS

The History of Ipswich

Town Hall, 1868, with its original array of ornamentation.

The History of Ipswich

1500 YEARS OF TRIUMPH & DISASTER

PETER BISHOP

UNICORN PRESS

TO
JACKIE AND SAM
my new daughters-in-law

By the same author: Grundisburgh: the history of a Suffolk village

First published in Great Britain 1995
by Unicorn Press, 21 Afghan Rd. London SW11 2QD

A catalogue record for this book is available at the British Library
ISBN 0 906290 10 4

Typeset by Create Publishing Services, Bath
Printed and bound in Great Britain by Bookcraft, Midsomer Norton
Jacket printed by The Balkerne Press, Colchester

Contents

Illustrations

Acknowledgements

My thanks are due to Mrs. Michael Cambridge for permission to reproduce photographs from the Suitall Collection; to Canon Keith Jones for permission to photograph details from the Smart Memorial in his church; to Dr. J. Blatchly for the sketch of Dykes Alexander, to Mr. Bob Malster for his photograph of a horse-tram, and to the Suffolk Record Office and the Ipswich Borough Council Museums and Galleries for the use of illustrations from their collections. I would also like to thank the staff of the Ipswich Record Office for their kindness and efficiency, and my wife, Helen, for her moral support, practical help, wise counsel, and constant patience.

From the Suitall Collection: Daundy's Cross, the Regatta, the Promenade, and the Victorial Memorial.

From Ipswich Museums and Galleries: Gainsborough's gardener, the proposed tunnel under Stoke Hill, the port of Ipswich from the gas holder; and details from: the crane at the Common Quay; the Tooleys' house; the Wet Dock from the Workhouse gardens; Henry Tooley; Samuel Ward; Samuel Kilderbee; and W. Woolaston.

The rest are from the *Suffolk Record Office* at Ipswich.

Introduction

THE OLD lady has seen better days. Her wrinkled face, none too clean, is plastered with tawdry make-up, and her fine clothes are darned and patched. A dirty river, Orwell and Gipping, formerly her life-blood, creeps neglected through steel embankments of industrial wasteland. Office blocks punctuate a skyline once commanded by the towers of her now redundant churches. Traffic signs have supplanted her many trees. Only at her heart, on Cornhill, is there any sense of the old style, of the confident beauty who has weathered the triumphs and disasters of fifteen hundred years.

This book attempts to tell the tale of those years. Ipswich was old when the Normans came, it was devastated like most places by the Black Death, and achieved great and sudden wealth under the Tudors when its enduring beacon of nonconformism was first ignited. It was overcome by sloth and corruption in the eighteenth century and by high-minded industrialism in the nineteenth. What strengths and weaknesses have survived these experiences, because they have survived, in buildings, ideas, customs and memories, have deep roots. They cannot be ignored. They have shaped the modern town, at least as much as we have ourselves. It would be nice to add that they have something to teach us, but history is a cruel storyteller, random and biased, more concerned with vice than virtue, folly than wisdom. The lesson is a general one: Ipswich has seen off fifty generations: it is safe from us.

The town was founded as a commercial centre, and commerce and industry, noble in their aims but often mean in their execution, are the unbroken themes of its history, linking us back through the centuries from Ransomes and Cobbolds, Bayleys and Barnards, Tooley, Harneys and the Bigots, to the legendary Gippa himself. Making money is competitive and time-consuming, and no great cathedral or similar works of combined effort were ever undertaken, whose clear merits might have preserved the town from the worst encroachments of modern living. The Ipswich we have inherited is a shaky structure in need of carefully renewal. Perhaps impatience is the danger now – the planners, with their grand designs and all-too-fallible optimism.

Interest in local history is a recent phenomenon. It is comforting to glimpse our ancestors against a familiar background, if only to see how their mistakes were made and how similar they were to ours. Ipswich is well endowed with records into which, since the Second World War, antiquarians have delved to great effect. Few subjects, from the Chaucers to the Cobbolds, medieval justice to swimming pools, have escaped their industry. My debt to all of them is correspondingly immense.

I have done some delving of my own, sometimes to verify secondary sources, and sometimes to unravel municipal minutiae which often proved too vague or incomplete to interest the general reader. Uncertainties have to be qualified, and too many of them destroy the story's flow. With a limit of 60,000 words to cover 1500 years, 40 words per year, I have tried to avoid that pitfall. Illustrations help. They say one picture is worth a thousand words, but a thousand pictures, without the meat of narrative, are not worth a million. They are the soufflé, not the main course. Moreover, the history of Ipswich is so much older than the oldest of them that they can give a false perspective. I hope this little book, for all its mistakes and inadequacies, may offer a fuller meal.

CHAPTER ONE

Rise and Fall

WUFFA and his men set foot on the Saxon Shore around 550, a band of marauding Swedes. Within two generations, his family, Kings of East Anglia, were the most powerful in southern England and, to judge from the contents of the great cenotaph at Sutton Hoo (probably for his grandson Redwald) one of the richest in Europe. Redwald's palace was at Rendlesham, while a dozen miles to the south-west, prospering under royal protection, was the *wick* or town which served it.

Gippa, the town's eponymous founder, sited his market on the northern shore of the Orwell at its lowest and shortest fordable crossing a few yards downstream from Stoke Bridge. Upstream, also on its north bank, just west of Stoke Bridge, the Orwell was joined by a branch or tributary, very short and flowing through the marshes which protected the town's western boundary. At some stage, taking its name from the town, this stream became known as the Gipping, a slimy concrete mouth now the only visible evidence of its existence. Today's Gipping, the river which rises beyond Stowmarket and at some mystic point becomes the Orwell, was once – certainly in 1340 – very sensibly called the Orwell for its whole length. The present mix-up between the two goes back at least to the fifteenth century. (They order this matter better in Massachusetts where the river that flows through Ipswich is called the Ipswich River.)

Nothing is known about Gippa, or Gipe, except perhaps that he was excessively prone to yawning. Names in those days were often formed from a man's most obvious, if not least agreeable, characteristic, and 'gipian' is the old English verb to yawn. 'Yawnsville', however, is an undignified translation for the name of Suffolk's county town, and there is an alternative explanation which denies Gippa ever existed and maintains that it comes from 'gipa', an opening (such as might describe an estuary) or a corner (as of an open mouth) like the sharp bend in the Orwell at Ipswich Dock.

The 'G' before 'i' in Gipe is silent, making the 'i' short, so his name would have been pronounced Yippa. In time – about a thousand years – spelling inevitably followed speech, and Gipeswick gave place to Ypswich.

Much of Redwald's wealth would have come from plundering his neighbours whose persons, animals, slaves and other bric-a-brac he looked to the merchants of Ipswich to trade for more prestigious items like wine and furs from the Rhineland and beyond. Commerce is a high-risk, high-reward occupation, and less enterprising folk earned a steadier living in the town as weavers, metal-bashers and potters.

It is the evidence of the last of these which is of most use to the historian. Ipswich at that time was arguably the main commercial centre in England, so that its potters were the first to acquire the latest technology from the continent; and pieces of Ipswich Ware are the earliest that have been discovered which were turned on a wheel and kiln-fired. Their remains have been found all over East Anglia, including the cenotaph at Sutton Hoo. And in the town itself, the locations of their many shards of grey, yellow or russet (cooking pots plus a few lamps and wine-jars) clearly delineate its earliest extent: north-south from Tower Ramparts to the Orwell and west-east from roughly Civic Drive and Franciscan Way to Upper and Lower Orwell Streets. The potters' quarter was at the town's eastern extremity, near Carr Street where kilns have been discovered.

These 150 acres – less a town than an encampment dotted at intervals with groups of thatched huts – may have been only seasonally inhabited. Certainly some families had orchards of apple, plum, cherry and raspberry whose stones and pips archaeologists have unearthed. Oyster shells, too, have been found, as well as eel, pike, trout and salmon bones, and perhaps only the fishing families were permanent residents.

Redwald believed in hedging his bets, and maintained both a pagan and a Christian altar at Rendlesham. It is probable the people of Ipswich were equally ambivalent. They had a largely pagan cemetery off the Hadleigh Road opposite Sainsbury's where sixth and seventh century bones of nearly 200 of them have been uncovered: the men with spears or javelins beside them, shields over their faces (and one small boy with his toy spear), the women with rings and broaches, together with necklaces of coloured paste or amber.

Christianity became a serious option under Sigebert, Redwald's son, and St Felix, his bishop. But Sigebert soon retired to a monastery,

Felix died about 650, and in the great plague of 663, the infant Church was all but strangled at birth.

Two hundred years later, after the martyrdom of King Edmund, a pagan ruled once more in East Anglia, a Danish bandit called Guthrum. He it was, no doubt, who gave Ipswich its defensive ditch and ramparts, and established on the Orwell a naval dockyard whence, in 885, his fleet would have sailed to defeat King Alfred in an engagement off Harwich. Guthrum's vessels had 30 oars aside, much bigger than Alfred's, who subsequently designed his ships with 60 aside, the original Royal Navy.

The Danes were soon driven out of East Anglia, and for another century Ipswich prospered in relative peace. Churches were built inside the ramparts, suburbs and more churches grew up outside, and a mint was established.

Leofric and Lifinge were the two minters named on the town's earliest discovered coin (about 973) bearing the head of Alfred's great-grandson, King Edgar. The presence of their names on the coinage was not vanity but a guarantee of its purity, redeemable by the removal of one of the offender's hands if it was not. Licences were obtainable only in London whence the minters collected the dies in person whenever the design was changed.

Minting became a growth industry following demand for coin to pay the new tax or geld raised in ever-increasing sums by Ethelred the Unready to buy off chronic waves of Danish invaders. The town was raided at least twice, the second time by Canute before he seized power in 1016. There were 15 minters in Ipswich during the reigns of Ethelred and Canute, and later between 5 and 10, until persistent debasement persuaded King John to close them down.

The coinage was based on the silver penny and the pound sterling: 12 pence to the shilling and 20 shillings to the pound, a system which remained unchanged for a thousand years until 1971. As an exceedingly rough guide, food prices have increased about a thousand times in that period, and a farm worker's pay nearly eight thousand,[1] the difference representing one measure of his improved standard of living over the millennium. The merchants and tradesmen of Ipswich have palpably done better than that.

Taxes, as we know, once introduced, are rarely dismantled, and the Domesday survey was ordered by William the Conqueror in 1086 chiefly to find out, after 20 years of progress, if he was getting enough.

1. These multipliers rapidly get out of date: in my book on Grundisburgh some years ago, I calculated the wage multiplier was under 6,000, at which level it rises 1,000 points for an 18 per cent pay rise.

As Ethelred's original valuations were often still in use, it was a reasonable assumption that he was not.

Ipswich was an exception. In 20 years its population had more than halved to around 1,000: 538 taxpaying households in 1066 and 210 in 1086, 100 of whom were too poor to pay more than a nominal penny a year. Nevertheless their combined tax and rent (the King was the town's chief landlord, so the distinction was nice one) was £40 a year. That was what the King received. The people paid a higher figure because the tax collection had been privatised, 'farmed out' to someone who could see a profit in it, in return for a guarantee that the King would get his £40 regardless. (There had obviously been a problem, and the Sheriff, as the King's agent, had agreed a reduction in the guarantee to £37.) Before the Conquest, the town's total bill had been only £15 plus 300 lbs of honey worth 90 pence in all, roughly today's price in real terms. It is a familiar picture of a once affluent generation crippled by high and prolonged taxation.

The minters likewise (their Saxon names crudely Normanised) whose licence fees before 1066 had aggregated £4 a year, were now charged £20, and in 1086 were £53 in arrears. No word of any reduction for them.

Ownership of people could be more lucrative than ownership of land, and in Ipswich two-thirds of these 'profits' of jurisdiction also went to the King. They comprised not only the fines imposed by the Courts which could be substantial (especially for murder where the man responsible for catching the culprit was liable if he failed) but also the feudal approximation of our stamp duties on birth, death, marriage and so on.

Domesday mentions 10 churches in Ipswich, 5 or possibly 6 within the ramparts and the rest in the suburbs. St Michael's, one of the ten, was probably replaced by the later church of St Nicholas where a carving remains, dated about 1050, depicting St Michael's fight with Dane the Dragon. The homes, gardens and orchards of the townspeople covered 40 acres: much of the rest appears to have been the glebe land of the churches.

In the Half Hundred of Ipswich (a Hundred being an administrative subdivision of the county, with that of Ipswich about half the usual size) were two farms and a manor. The town itself was in the middle of the Half Hundred whose boundaries closely coincided with those of the modern conurbation, the A14 marking its western and southern limits. The meeting place, and tax collection point, of the

St. Michael and Dane the dragon.

Half Hundred was St Margaret's Green, long known by its Danish name of Thingstead.

To the south-east, the later Holywell's Park, was the King's farm of 480 acres, occupied at Domesday by 24 families who owned 48 oxen between them which they hired out as six ploughteams to the farm which had only one of its own. There were 13 sheep on the farm, 7 goats, 3 cows and a pack-horse, less than half the numbers of 20 years previously.

The other farm, north of the King's and half its size was astride the Foxhall Road. It was held by the Conqueror's son-in-law, O'Bret Alan. There were only 7 families here, presumably the owners of the 3 ploughteams on which it was wholly dependent.

The single manor of 720 acres with its assortment of feudal rights belonging to St Peter's church in Ipswich and was held after the Conquest by Richard FitzGilbert of Clare. There were 15 acres in the town itself, but the main estate, where 100 acres were in dispute with the manor of Bramford, was probably off the Norwich Road near Broke Hall. Forty-four families lived there in 1086, compared to 37 when the Normans arrived. Thanks to its connection with FitzGilbert, it was the only part of Ipswich to have prospered since 1066, and its value had trebled.

South of Stoke Bridge, already 100 years old at the Conquest, the road led up to Stoke's manor and church, long possessed by the Abbey of Ely. Its 360 acres were cultivated by 24 households and there was a water mill by the bridge. Its tax rating seems to have been very favourable – just 4 pence out of every pound paid by the manor, farms and town of Ipswich.

In Saxon times, two-thirds of the jurisdiction of the town and the whole of its larger farm had been the property of Queen Edith, estranged wife of Edward the Confessor, while her brother, Earl Gyrth, had the other third and the smaller farm. After 1066 Gyrth was replaced by Early Ralf, followed by his son and heir, also Ralf, whose lands were forfeited after his rebellion in 1075. Then O'Bret Alan got the farm, but probably not the jurisdiction. The explanation of the town's Domesday plight may be that, lured by promises, it had supported the younger Ralf.

CHAPTER TWO

The Charter

ROGER BIGOT, the Domesday sheriff, had risen from being a small and obscure landowner in Normandy to one of the largest and most powerful in England. His name implies he was an obstinate man; and his refusal, in the face of the town's 80 per cent decline in earning capacity, to adapt the King's financial demands, makes it unlikely his ideas of justice were any more enlightened. Indeed, if it was he who received the one-third share of the profits of jurisdiction forfeited by Earl Ralf, he had a strong incentive to let the full rigour of feudal law take its course.

His seat of power in Ipswich was the castle, a wooden Norman construction, appropriately sited (as it is now thought) near the present Police Station on the western edge of town. It was demolished in 1176 on the orders of Henry II after Hugh Bigot, Roger's son, having changed sides four times in the course of the Civil War between Stephen and Matilda, had joined yet another rebellion.

Earlier, during one of the periods when he was supporting Matilda, Bigot had been successfully besieged in the castle by Stephen, whose troops the town would have been expected to house, and perhaps to feed, meanwhile. Medieval royalty lived in the saddle, and visitations could be ruinous to their hosts (£50 a night was a going rate in Domesday) even when no fighting was involved.

It may have been the memory of such expenses, not to mention the behaviour of the Bigots, which persuaded the next generation to open negotiations with the Crown for the grant of their first Charter, sealed by King John on 25 May 1200. Others were to follow, expanded and amended by successive monarchs, but they were all based on this one. Tradition has it that King John added a gift to his: the still-surviving replica of a Saxon Horn of Justice, to be blown round the town at midnight on the eve of every session of the Great Court.

The old land tax or geld was everywhere being supplemented by better revenue earners like customs duties. That of Ipswich, which was still around £35 a year, had been in arrears for some time; and the Charter was conditional both on its being brought up-to-date and on agreement to pay an additional £5 in future, the collection to be in the hands of the town authorities, not the Sheriff.

The Charter also empowered the burgesses of Ipswich not only to refuse to have troops quartered on them (but would that ever be a prudent veto?) but also, in civil and petty criminal cases to administer their own Courts of Justice. Moreover, Ipswich merchants, whose business transactions were now exempt from tolls throughout the country, could only be prosecuted in no doubt more amenable Ipswich Courts, regardless of where the dispute arose.

The government of the town was transferred from the Sheriff into the hands of two Bailiffs – senior and junior in case of dispute – chosen annually by the whole town at a Great Court. Under them were four similarly-chosen coroners, law officers, who were supposed to act as a check on the Bailiffs; an optimistic supposition when at the first election two of the coroners were the two Bailiffs. Bailiffs and coroners then appointed an electoral college of four men from each parish to chose twelve 'portmen' for life. Unsurprisingly all four coroners found themselves voted portmen.

It took several months to settle the design of the town seal, possibly the unsuitable compromise of a committee: a man o'war with fighting castles fore and aft, far removed from the small coastal vessels of the Ipswich merchants, and more imposing even than the Dutch merchantmen which monopolised the town's trade at that time with the continent. The seal's chief interest today is that it depicts the oldest known example of a rudder fixed to the ship's stern-post in place of the usual steering oar on the starboard side.

On the back of the seal is the church on Cornhill of St Mildred, an eighth-century Kentish abbess whose remains ended up in Holland, a piece of which some merchant possibly brought back to Ipswich as a relic. By now, however, the church seems to have become the seat of the Great Court and the town's judicial and administrative centre – hence its appearance on the seal. Somewhere in the building, a chapel was still reserved for the saint until the Reformation.

The Bailiffs' first task was to codify the town's by-laws which had evolved over the years. They called the result of these efforts Le Domesday, their aim doubtless being to discourage appeals: the Conqueror's great Survey had become so nicknamed for achieving this very objective.

All this was gone over with impressive deliberation, and mass meetings were held throughout the summer. Although the Charter covered the Half Hundred of Ipswich as well as the town, the meetings took place not in the Thingstead (St Margaret's Green) but in the churchyard nearby of St Mary le Tower, no doubt to emphasis their solemnity. At the second meeting, all officials having been chosen, a Bible was held aloft, and all present stretched their hands towards it (one imagines the right hand, in a sort of Hitler salute) and swore in chorus to obey their new masters. For 461 years a similar oath was sworn every Whit Tuesday afternoon by every freeman between the ages of 16 and 60 at meetings of the four leets or wards into which the town had long been divided. Ipswich thus exchanged the autocracy of the Sheriff for an oligarchy of four – in theory six – plus the

St. Mildred's, Cornhill.

portmen, at one remove their appointees. But it was a step in the right direction.

There are no better gamekeepers than ex-poachers. Le Domesday was devised by such men, and in 1204 new ramparts, with 20 foot ditches beyond, were started outside the old defences under their guidance. It was another century before they obtained permission to encircle the town with a stone wall (and then they never got round to doing so) but meanwhile the Saxon earthworks were evidently in no condition to keep out anybody, specifically at that time the smugglers.

More efficient administration put a greater value on burgess-status in Ipswich, and the records show a steady stream of local landlords applying for the freedom of the town with its consequent exemption from tolls for their produce. Among the first were the Bigots, who paid the equivalent of about £3 (an ox, a bull, 9 cwt of wheat and 9 cwt of barley) for the privilege, in addition to an annual rent of 4 pence for Bigot's Wharf beside Stoke Bridge. Most people paid less initially for the freedom, usually between 12 and 15 shillings in wheat and live-stock plus around 5 shillings a year thereafter. Less commercially-minded landowners could have honorary status of out-burgesses.

Le Domesday's regulations regarding the conduct of foreign merchants, the town's lifeblood, were commendably explicit, and Mercantile Courts sat for their convenience at the port, on the foreshore at low tide. Everyone thus had an instant reminder to keep it brief. Each foreigner had a local 'hostman' through whom – for a commission – his business must be transacted, and in whose warehouse his goods were stored. He himself had to lodge on his hostman's property, often one of the hostelries in Tavern Street with warehouse adjoining.

Like most restrictive practices, the origin of this arrangement was doubtless sound, to make an Ipswich man responsible in the event of malpractice by a possibly elusive stranger. Over time, it developed into jobs for the boys and an acceptance of the idea that if anyone was going to benefit from malpractice, it might as well be a local merchant.

Few of the activities of man have changed as little in detail as that of the market place, the arena – they say – of money made rather than earned, of brokers and rumour, of feast and famine, it doesn't matter which, so long as prices move; where controls exist only to be manipulated, and the transparency of the official markets is merely a cover for more profitable private transactions. Ipswich was probably no more chaotic than other towns of the period, or indeed than the City of London today, and its government fought a daily battle on behalf of the shopkeepers and stallholders in the street-markets against the rich pirate-merchants who operated outside them.

Private deals were forbidden but widespread. Hostmen, for example, who were typically portmen and often ex-bailiffs and coroners, reckoned to make a 25 per cent commission on their imported goods by dealing direct with consumers away from the regular markets. (Doubtless on exports their margins were narrower: the customers, the foreign 'guests', were too strong: they had long disliked the exchange control which compelled them to balance their sales against local purchases, and this had to be relaxed to allow them to remit half their earnings in cash.)

By the mid-century, the mood, not to say idealism, of 1200 had evaporated. Only the measured prescripts of Le Domesday stood between Ipswich and anarchy when in 1271 John Le Blake, the town clerk, who in that job would have known more than most about official corruption, and was alleged to have been sucked into it himself, disappeared with the great work, never to be seen again.

For twelve years the authorities did nothing about this convenient loss which must have considerably increased the range of their public, as well as their private, discretion. Then one day a riot broke out in the County Court sitting in Ipswich, and the Sheriff himself was held for a ransom of two barrels of wine. No doubt it was the opportunity the Sheriff had been waiting for, and the town's constitution was suspended in favour of direct Crown rule. This lasted for eight years when reforms were introduced in 1291: a new Domesday was put together from memories of the old, and a new Council established, supplementing existing officials, of 24 men elected by the whole town. At the same time, under a fresh Charter, the tax due from Ipswich to the King was raised from £40 to £60 a year.

The Council of 24, some of whom, as one would expect, appear to have been healthily anti-establishment, did nothing much for thirty years until perhaps fear of another bout of Crown rule, tough, bureaucratic and ruinous to trade, goaded them to action.

The Council issued an Ordnance attacking the bailiffs, Thomas Le Rente and Thomas Stace. Self-made men, they had both held office almost continuously since 1297. (Le Rente had earlier been one of the 'wise men' helping to reconstruct Le Domesday.) They were accused of (i) getting themselves elected by a tiny, self-perpetuating clique (ii) taking high fees as bribes which disadvantaged those who couldn't afford them (iii) using the town seal improperly to sell freedoms for their own account and (iv) raising excessive taxes to spend on themselves.

Three proposals were consequently adopted at a full meeting of the town: depose the Bailiffs; appoint key-holders to the Town Hutch or Chest which contained the seal; and allow new Bailiffs to nominate a chamberlain each, 'two sufficient persons of the inferior sort', to collect the taxes and keep proper accounts. Clearly it was intended the chamberlains should be on friendly, but not intimate, terms with their masters, and they were given the right to dine with the Bailiffs every Sunday, or take cash in lieu. Even so, within a few years, at least one of them became a bailiff himself. In a mercantile society, class barriers are difficult to maintain.

Le Rente and Stace fought back in the Courts and obtained royal Letters of protection, to no avail. Their homes were attacked and ransacked, and one of Stace's sons was murdered. Le Rente, pressed by creditors and fined £333 in 1322 by the King's Exchequer for concealment of customs duties, died soon after. By 1330 Stace too was dead.

The tax rolls of 1282, when the population of Ipswich inside the ramparts was about 3,000 – treble the low point of 1086 – record the moveable possessions of 280 households: 39 had assets of £10 or more and 57 under £1, a value which would have put them among the wealthiest taxpayers of many a village nearby. Among the poorest men on the list was William Le Gardener, worth 80 pence, the lowest level at which the tax operated. The two richest were Hugo Golding, a draper, with property totalling £163 and Philip Harneys with £117 (£20 in household goods, the rest in merchandise of millstones – curiously the official monopoly of portmen – plus iron, timber, wine and farm produce). Ipswich now was a relatively poor town, and ranked below Bury, Yarmouth and King's Lynn.

Harneys was lord of a manor in Ashbocking, 8 miles away. Was he one of the numerous landlords who had become Ipswich freemen and set up an establishment there for trading purposes? Or was he, as is more likely, a merchant who had made good and acquired aspirations as a country gentleman, an enduring aspect of commercial tradition?

The population of the rest of Suffolk is thought to have roughly doubled since the Conquest. So, as a consequence, had prices, but not wages. Only the merchants could protect their income from inflation. But farm workers, too, were tempted into Ipswich in search of a better life, especially after the bad harvests of 1315–21. Some of them were traced or spotted by their feudal lords and sent home. There were perhaps as many as 300 houses in the suburbs by now, mostly in St Matthew's parish and along the estuary in St Clement's.

The town was still very much a rural community. Twenty households owned horses, and not a few had cows, pigs and hens. Pigs roamed everywhere and were a constant nuisance. Some people even had oxen, while many merchants held large stores of wheat. Thirty families had interests in fishing boats and ships, the largest being valued at £10, a small coastal vessel. A barge of 30 oars built by Harneys for the King cost £200.

Ipswich, of course, was an important entrepot for wool. This was subject to royal customs duty, and smuggling it abroad was a popular pastime. Eleven men about this period faced prosecution for doing so but were acquitted for lack of evidence.

Once, for reasons of foreign policy, the King banned all wool exports from the town, and bought up the crop himself, having mortgaged the Queen's jewels for £2,500 to a local pawnbroker. It had been a perfect year for sheep so the price was exceptionally low. Five years later when it was higher, he sold the lot and redeemed the jewels. Meantime, much of the wool was stored in a range of warehouses along the west side of Bolton Lane where there was also a machine for weighing it.

Although some merchants specialised, the majority, like Philip Harneys, were prepared to deal in anything which promised a good profit. In an age of bad smells, and meat far from fresh, spices were important, and Thomas Le Spicer's stock was highly valued at almost £7. There were as many as 20 tanners and skinners, mostly by the marshes north-west of Portman's Meadow where since 1200 the portmen had had the exclusive right to graze their horses. Some of the four dyers and the dozen or so cloth merchants rented space in the ramparts' ditches to dry and stretch their wares; one of them held nearly £8 worth of woad and ashes for his trade.

The tax rolls (whose seven skins it would be nice to think had been supplied by William Le Percheminener, the parchment specialist) mention 5 shoemakers, 6 blacksmiths, a goldsmith, a glover and a carpenter, but there must have been others, too poor to appear as taxpayers. Armaments were represented by a solitary maker of cross-bows. Only 2 weavers are recorded; like carding and spinning, this was a cottage industry carried out by the poorest families, often in villages

The Medieval Shambles.

nearby, who were sometimes tempted to use their employers' stock as loan collateral.

Probably since Gippa's day, Cornhill had been the main market place of Ipswich, dominated by St Mildred's church on the site of the present Town Hall. The town centre as a whole was unchanged in layout from what it had been centuries earlier, and largely from what it remains today. The meat market stretched from Shambles in Cornhill's south-east corner (today's site of our old Post Office) along the western half of Tavern Street; poultry was at the corner of Tower Street. In front of the Shambles was a stake for bull-baiting, an activity which until the eighteenth century was thought to improve the beef. There was a fine for selling meat which had not been baited for an hour on the day of slaughter.

Beyond the Poultry, between the top of Dial Lane and St Lawrence Street, was the Vintry. Wine, not beer, was the tipple of the taverns. It was one of the very oldest imports of Ipswich, and having mysteriously ceased about the time of Guthrum, had been brought back by the Normans. Beer, without hops, was brewed at under a quarter penny a pint (50p today) by a few ale-wives in St Clement's parish.

The cloth market was in St Lawrence Street and the fish market in the central section of Buttermarket, with cheese and butter to its west. To the south, at the top of Silent Street, was the town's chief dunghill. In 1447, at the beginning of the cloth export boom, the cloth market had to move to a larger site beside and behind the Town Hall.

Originally, the town's Great Court sat as the Portmansmote in the Leadenhall or Hall of Pleas, probably near the Northgate and the Thingstead, before taking over St Mildred's on Cornhill. The County Court was outside the ramparts to emphasise the town's independence, and is thought to have been east of the Lower Wash (Lower Orwell Street) beside which the Cauldwell brook flowed from beyond the Woodbridge Road into the Orwell. Another stream, rising in Christchurch Park, ran parallel a few yards to the west along the side of Brook Street, the town's main north-south highway from the earliest times. As traffic increased, Stoke Bridge was often closed to heavy vehicles, and an area was set aside by Bigot's Wharf where they could wait for low tide before using the ford.

Although King John's Charter had not mentioned the matter, it had always been assumed that the jurisdiction of Ipswich extended over the Orwell estuary. The fisheries and oyster beds along its banks were regulated by the town, and disputes with riparian landlords, usually the Bigots, settled in its Courts. The fish traps and weirs were sometimes argued to be illegal and a danger to shipping, to which from time to time the Bigots added cruder strong-arm hazards to persuade merchantmen to switch their trade to Harwich which they also owned.

Suddenly in 1338 that town obtained a royal Charter which gave it the dues and jurisdiction of the 'Port of Orwell'. No financial panic of modern times can compare with that which this news must have created among the merchants of Ipswich. But the Bailiffs acted immediately, and within a few weeks the status quo was restored. The King happened to be in Walton near Felixstowe at the time, preparing for the first expedition against France of the Hundred Years War – temporarily filling Ipswich with rowdy archers from the Welsh borders while they waited to board the armada gathering in the Orwell.

Six years later, an Assize judge had occasion to complain rather childishly to the King or Sheriff about the behaviour of some sailors in his Court at Ipswich. He had adjourned it for dinner, and the sailors (defendants or witnesses?) held a mock trial while they waited, 'fining' him for taking too long over his meal. Possibly the Bailiffs angered him further by making light of the whole affair; they were certainly reluctant to punish the sailors. Anyway, Harwich had its revenge for loss of its Orwell jurisdiction, and for the next few months Ipswich again suffered the inconvenience of direct Crown rule.

But soon war and rivalries receded before a more serious threat, the Black Death and the plagues which followed over the next century.

CHAPTER THREE

Holy Ipswich

CORPUS CHRISTI was inaugurated by the Pope as one of the great festivals of the Church in 1264. It became the day (the Thursday after Trinity Sunday) when, in clerical circles, tonsures were renewed and beards shaved. A day to remember. In Ipswich, since 1325, it had been the feast day of the Merchants' Guild.

Established under the Charter of King John, the Guild in the early years was effectively an arm of local government, and in theory another check on the power of the Bailiffs. It held the receipts from the purchase of freedoms and operated a Closed Shop for everyone wanting exemption from tolls. Its five controlling aldermen were usually portmen.

The Guild's main concern was the regulation of trade, although a good part of its substantial funds was devoted to charity. Its church was the main church of the town, St Mary le Tower.

At the beginning of May 1325, the Priors of Holy Trinity (on today's site of Christchurch Mansion) and of St Peter and Paul (incorporating St Peter's church by Bigot's Wharf) had the idea that the guild should be dedicated to Corpus Christi and that, weather permitting, there should be an annual procession through the town from Holy Trinity to St Peter and Paul and back; and, in alternate years, in the reverse direction. Time was short, and details were rapidly agreed at a meeting between priors and merchants in St Margaret's church.

The two priories were exclusive independent foundations of Augustinian Canons, an order originating from secular cathedral clergy. They tended to recruit novices from among the gentry who often arrived with useful endowments. Around this time there were 8 Canons at Holy Trinity (sometimes referred to as Christchurch) and about 13 at St Peter and Paul. They had grown rich since their establishment in Ipswich about 150 years ago, and now between them held the patronage of most churches in the town. The former had an

Tower Street, with St. Mary le Tower and St. Lawrence's.

income of £136 a year in 1291 and the latter £82. The crusades had been especially rewarding, when many young men, keen to raise cash in order to take part, had mortgaged their lands to the priories and never returned.

The procession started at 9 am, taking a route via St Mary le Tower to Cornhill where possibly the play or pageant was performed; thereafter along Buttermarket to St Lawrence's, the weavers' church, south past St Stephen's, and down Brook Street to St Peter and Paul. Then back to Holy Trinity and the lunch-feast on Cornhill.

Later in the day, surely much later, there was a ceremony in the chancel of St Mary le Tower where 13 paupers, representing Christ and the 12 apostles, were given a penny each and had their feet washed by a couple of priests. The floor was then strewn with straw before a Requiem Mass on the Sunday for the souls of former members. Everyone wore black for that.

By about 1350 most of the 40-odd crafts had followed the merchants' example and banded into their own guilds: weavers, dyers, carpenters, barbers and others into St Thomas's guild with a chapel in St Lawrence's church; plumbers, masons, saddlers and pewterers into

St George's whose pre-Conquest chapel stood outside the ramparts in St George's Street north of Westgate; tailors were under St John, and smiths of all kinds under St Eligius, a seventh-century French goldsmith.

One by one over the years the craft guilds were admitted to the procession, and an order of precedence established. Each craft-group carried a banner usually depicting its patron saint, although the fish-mongers had a dolphin and the merchants themselves (a convincing representation of Corpus Christi being perhaps difficult to achieve) a merchant ship.

The merchants, followed by the craftsmen, led the way. Behind them came the Blessed Sacrament borne by priests from the two priories and surrounded by the shining pates and chins of the other clergy. Next were the Bailiffs and the rest of the town officials. The five aldermen of the Merchants' Guild made up the rear.

As the Guild's political involvement, and its wealth, diminished, numbers at these festivities declined. That may have been why the craftsmen were invited to join. By 1500, penalties were in place to encourage attendance. Prominent men offered, or were persuaded, to finance the dramatic performances, but there is no word of any of the rivalry among them which is apparent elsewhere. (That came later, in the seventeenth century, when the whole ceremony had degenerated into a private dinner party for local worthies and their wives.)

All the craft guilds had joined by 1490 when details of the feast are extant. The cost was nicely calculated at 6 pence for a man and 4 pence for his wife, and, as the total seems to have been about £7, at least 300 people attended. In addition to wine, beer and bread, they consumed 10 lambs, 2 calves, 16 pigs, 70 chickens and 100 pigeons. Perhaps the clergy got in free to swell the numbers. The cook's pay was 20 pence and that of his or her assistants up to 3 pence each. Musicians were provided, but only remunerated afterwards by passing round the hat.

The food was prepared in the former St Mildred's, by now known as the Guildhall. The church's little spire had been taken, or had fallen, down, its roof remodelled, and a floor added which was entered through a new main doorway via a steep flight of steps from Cornhill. In 1393, a brick annexe had been built on its east side on a strip of land donated by the Prior of Holy Trinity. And after the Reformation when, deprived of religious significance, guild procession and feast had become sporadic, this curious amalgam of ecclesiastical and dom-estic gothic was renamed the Town Hall.

Neither merchants nor craftsmen dominated the Corpus Christi procession, but priests. Clergy resident within a 15 mile radius had a standing invitation to attend, and were fined if they failed to do so; a simple matter, since their livings were mostly held by one of the priories or by a local landlord, usually himself a burgess. In addition, beside the priories' 20-odd Canons, there were the town's own Dominicans, Franciscans and Carmelites, by 1325 at least 100.

These three orders of mendicant friars – Black, Grey and White respectively – had all set up houses in Ipswich between about 1260 and 1280, the years of disillusion when Le Domesday disappeared and official insolence became endemic. At a time in which materialism everywhere was rife and the gap widening fast between rich and poor, the friars were the Church's new battalions, trained in a potent and novel weapon, the art of preaching. What they preached was simply that all men were created equal.

Unlike the Canons, they were mostly from poor backgrounds and lived, as their title implies, entirely on charity. They flourished in Ipswich. During their first 200 years of existence, all three had reason to enlarge their houses several times, presumably because their numbers were growing.

Blackfriars, founded by Henry III, was the greatest in extent, and its church of St Mary said to be the largest in town. Its house was situated in the rectangle of Foundation Street, Orwell Place, Lower Orwell Street and Star Lane, with an eastward projection over the rampart ditch. There were 22 priests in 1277, and more than double 20 years later. The Greyfriars' community (about 30 in 1291) who were on the other side of town, near today's Franciscan Way, was the smallest of the three, and the most beloved. The Whitefriars lived between Buttermarket and the Dunghill. They were the intellectual elite among the friars and considered the most eloquent. Their theological disputes with higher authority sometimes got them into trouble: one was told to go and fast in Paris, and another to lecture as a penance in London.

The preachers, one may be sure, were not slow to point the moral of the two great events to hit the town in the fourteenth century, the Black Death in 1349 and Peasant's Revolt in 1381, even though the latter was in part the result of that very preaching.

The Whitefriars, who may also have been more left-wing than the other two, in 1381 rather foolishly entertained Edmund Brounfield of Bury Abbey, the peasants' favoured candidate for its vacant position of abbot. And soon afterwards, a mob, led by a Harkstead farmer and the Parson of Bucklesham, attacked Ipswich itself; they ransacked St

Stephen's Rectory and the homes of two MP's, stealing £100 worth of merchandise from one of them who happened to be a poll-tax collector. They also attacked for some reason the residence of the Archdeacon of Suffolk, an absentee Italian Cardinal, perhaps on the site of the house built 100 years later by Archdeacon Pykenham, whose grand gateway can still be seen in Northgate Street. Father Brounfield ended up in the Tower of London, while the Harkstead farmer only escaped the gallows by turning King's Evidence.

The town had two leper or isolation hospitals in the fourteenth century, a reminder of the background to its other problems: St Leonard's in the Wherstead Road and the Hospital of St Mary Magdalen and St James in the eastern suburbs. The latter, closed down at the Reformation, was under the mastership of the Rector of St Helen's with its quite separate chapel dedicated to St Edmund 'Pountenay', a former Archbishop of Canterbury who had retired to Pontigny Abbey in Burgundy and was canonised in 1248.

It was in the cemetery of this chapel, just north of Blackfriars, that 106 fourteenth and fifteenth century skeletons have been unearthed. That was the era of plagues, so their evidence may be gloomier than the previous norm: 45 per cent had died between the ages of 12 and 25, and 30 per cent between 26 and 40; only 11 per cent had lived past 40. The average height of adults was 5 foot 8 for men and 5 foot 5 for women. The tallest man was 5 foot 11.

No other English town of its size is said to have preserved more medieval churches than Ipswich, a testimony to the thoroughness of its Victorian reconstructors, if not to the enduring piety of its people. The earliest remaining fabric in most cases dates from the century and a half after the Black Death. Indeed, the shock of the plague and the competitiveness of merchants were surely factors in their building or enlargement. Other reasons were the introduction of bell-ringing (still so evocative of the period) requiring towers, and the cult of the rood, or crucifix, requiring taller buildings for its screen and loft.

Of the Saxon churches mentioned in the Domesday survey, five names survive today. They were probably of wood; in the following century the Normans would have rebuilt them in stone, and added others. Three collapsed in the great storm of 1287.

When St Margaret's roof was raised in the fifteenth century by the addition of its clerestory, its low tower evidently was not (or not enough) and only achieved its present height in 1871. It was founded by the Augustinian Canons as a parochial substitute for the old church of Holy Trinity which had been incorporated into their priory.

Other Victorian improvements were notably less successful. St Mary le Tower, St Mary Stoke and St Stephen's, all Saxon foundations, were smartened up and altered almost beyond recognition. A similar fate befell the churches of Saints Helen, Clement and Matthew. St Mary le Tower, which is referred to as such in Domesday, and sometimes in later documents as St Mary-at-the-Steeple, was probably unique in the early days in actually possessing a tower. The modern one, like that of St Lawrence, is a particularly striking example of Victorian elaboration. To be fair to the Victorians, the churches by then were in a desperate state: the spire of St Mary le Tower had fallen down 200 years earlier and not been replaced, and 'ugly yellow stucco' held up the walls of most of the others.

St Lawrence's, also a Domesday church, whose fine interior survived the improvers, was rebuilt around 1440 by the families of a pair of drapers, Bottold and Baldwyn. Before the tower's reconstruction in 1882, its old clock had stuck out at a right-angle over Dial Lane, hence its name-change from Cooks' Row where meat pies were sold. The

St. Margaret's, 1865, before the tower was raised.

fifth Domesday church was St Peter's: it was rebuilt by the Priory Canons in the fourteenth century, enlarged by Wolsey in the sixteenth and by Gilbert Scott in the nineteenth.

St Mary Elms, called St Saviour's until the fourteenth century, was first built by the Normans. Its Tudor tower was constructed of bricks said to be surplus from Wolsey's school. St Mary Quay dates from about 1450 when the richest merchants began to build their homes near the river. And Star Lane, between St Mary Quay and Blackfriars, dedicated to St Mary, is surely named from the old hymn to Our Lady 'Hail, Star of the Sea'. As already mentioned, St Nicholas's with its memorial to Danish aggression was probably on the site of the Domesday St Michael's.

On 7 January 1297, Princess Elizabeth, Edward I's 14 year old daughter, got married in Ipswich. The widowed King, and presumably the Princess, arrived on 23 December. They were joined by the Princess's elder sister, the Duchess of Brabent and her brother Prince Edward, the later Edward II. For the next fortnight free food was distributed daily among the poor, reckoned to average 500, or one-eighth of the population of town and suburbs. It seems to have cost 1½ pence per day per head, roughly a day's wages. Numbers varied considerably: on the first day, a Sunday, only 140 turned up, on the next, Christmas Day, 200, and thereafter – probably as the word got around – usually 700.

Another £35 was spent on alms for the poor, some of it by tossing coins into the crowd from the priory porch of St Peter and Paul where the royal party were staying. The bridegroom, the Count of Holland, spent the week before the wedding at the King's expense in Colchester with nine Dutch attendants.

The friars, too, received free meals over the four days of Christmas at a daily cost of over a shilling a head, plus a further sixpennyworth each for the actual day of the wedding.

There were some problems over jewellery: the Duchess of Brabent didn't like what her father had ordered from London, and sent it all back; the pearl necklace, part of the King's wedding present to his daughter, failed to arrive; and one of the Princess's two golden coronets studded with emeralds, rubies and pearls, which had cost her father £50, so annoyed the King – perhaps already in a bad temper – that he threw it into the fire. That was just a day or two before she was due to wear it at the wedding of her friend Eleanor de Burgo, on the Wednesday before her own. The coronet was rescued, but minus an emerald and a ruby which evidently someone had been swift enough to pocket. Two fresh stones were luckily found and fitted. The Princess's other coronet, worth £90, was a plain gold one for the royal wedding itself.

There was also a last-minute panic over the trousseau. A house was rented and 35 tailors installed to work round the clock until it was properly finished. As their foreman received his bonus for overtime, one assumes it was.

The King's accounts, so detailed for most expenses – he was notoriously careful over money – make no mention of the food consumed at the wedding feast. Perhaps it was provided by his hosts. The costs of the entertainers, however, and their numbers, are well documented. There appear to have been 11 fiddlers, 2 trumpeters, 2

The Madonna of Ipswich at Nettuno.

harpists and a drummer, plus around 20 assorted 'minstrels', as well as 7 players, 2 conjurors and one dancer calling herself Matilda Makejoie. Ironically her wage of 2 shillings was charged to Prince Edward who really preferred boys. When it was all over, bride and groom sailed away towards the sunrise and Holland.

The marriage service took place in the little chapel of Our Lady of Grace, otherwise known as Our Lady of Ipswich, a celebrated shrine for pilgrims and the most venerated in the town. It was situated at the north-east corner of Lady Lane facing the Westgate.

The Virgin's gilded statue stood in a tabernacle of silver and gilt, its feet in silver slippers, its cloak hanging from a golden collar. One of her relics was contained in a piece of crystal. The statue was believed to have the power of miracles. Sir Thomas More witnessed one in 1515 when a 13 year old girl was cured of blasphemy. Catherine of Aragon visited the shrine twice in the summer of 1517, and Henry VIII himself heard Mass there in 1522.

In 1538, at the Reformation, the statue was dispatched secretly by boat to London and supposedly burned at Chelsea. But there is a persistent tradition in Italy that it was spirited away by some English sailors who in about 1550 were shipwrecked south of Rome near the little town of Nettuno where, no longer miraculous, it can still be seen.

CHAPTER FOUR

Dirt Books

GIPPA'S shrewd eye to environment has stood Ipswich in good stead, not only for mercantile and defensive purposes but also, as its prosperity grew, for the no less important conveniences of sanitation. The Cauldwell brook to the east, the little Gipping (or whatever it was called from time to time) to the west, the smaller stream flowing beside Brook Street through the town centre, all provided a swift and efficient sewage service into the cleansing tidal waters of the Orwell.

There was at least one pit or dunghill near each of them: the large one below Buttermarket was called the Colehill, and that to the east of Orwell Place, outside the ramparts, the Coldunghill or Warwick Pits. There was another to the south, close to the Public Lavatories off Fore Street which date from before 1500. Most houses had their own, or a shared, privy. One sported an iron grill over a convenient stream.

Upstream on the Cauldwell brook was the Common Wash, while further up again a wooden conduit led water, strictly for drinking only, to a basin at the top of St Lawrence Street. Private individuals were also permitted to pipe water from the rivers into their homes, more convenient than recourse to one of the town's numerous wells. And the gutters which ran down the middle of the streets and were regularly clogged up with butchers' offal, oyster shells and other matter, could be sluiced down when necessary by the rivers' water.

With its gardens, orchards, churchyards and cloisters – and by modern standards a tiny population – the centre of Ipswich in the middle ages had a spacious air. Its main streets, amply bordered by grass and wide enough by law for two wagons to pass, were narrowed only gradually by surreptitious encroachment; and what began as a modest projection for a porch or a bay window or a buttress, developed in time into the building of new houses whose front elevations trespassed flagrantly on the public highway. One man put a couple of posts several feet into the road outside his home so that he could sit between them watching the world go by, unmolested by traffic: he was told he could still do so if he put them a bit further back. Another trick, for those with land adjoining the rampart ditches, was to plant a hedge along their boundary a few feet outside it. In most cases the relaxed official reaction was to fine the culprit a few pennies and then charge him an annual rent.

Fines generally, even for nastier offences, were lenient. William Chambers had to pay a penalty of 6 pence (about £15 today) for dumping 14 wagon-loads of muck, presumably the contents of his cess-pit, into the town ditch near Tower Ramparts; and even the Holy Trinity Canons were once had up for causing similar refuse to be deposited in the street. This was frequently done in streets near the dunghills, no doubt because it was easier than manoeuvring the cart right up to the mound itself. A common penalty for that in the fifteenth century was a shilling.

Later, in 1541, parish Scavengers were 'elected' to supervise the whole messy business. Later still, after a sour comment by Queen Elizabeth, more serious efforts were made to clean up the town, and the streets were paved, something many places had done years before. Nevertheless, by 1900 the debris of over a thousand years had raised the level of Cornhill and Tavern Street by more than 5 feet.

All these matters were dealt with and noted down by officials ('Headboroughs') in what they called their Dirt Books. History is made up of Dirt Books or their equivalent, the register of the crimes, follies and misfortunes of otherwise unmemorable lives; and our knowledge of everyday affairs in medieval Ipswich is largely derived from the bald decrees of authority against misbehaviour and the anodyne proceedings of the Courts of Justice. The law-abiding, like the hygienic, have left fainter traces.

Perhaps the best known is the case of John Chaucer, father of the poet. John's own father and his aunt Agnes had been separate lessees of two hostelries at the bottom of Tower Street on either corner of its junction with Tavern Street. The father died, and John, still a boy and with solid financial expectations, went to live in London with his mother, or step-mother, and her new husband.

About the same time Aunt Agnes, too, got remarried to a man called Geoffrey Stace, son of the discredited Bailiff, who was soon to become a Bailiff himself. In the winter of 1324, these two abducted young John and brought him back to Ipswich in order to marry him off to Agnes's daughter Joan, and thus consolidate the family business.

Somehow they were stopped and the case came to Court. Their

The Westgate from outside the town.

defence was that (a) John had come willingly and (b) being 14 years old and able both to measure cloth and count up to 18, he was legally of age under an Ipswich by-law. Point (a) was successfully disputed – (b) was true – and John was awarded damages of £250, or over £100,000 in modern currency. Thereafter he was packed off to a spell in the army.

The Staces appealed, and whether they ever paid the £250 is uncertain, although we do know both sides of the family later became intimate again: John named his son Geoffrey (the poet) after his step-uncle Stace, while cousin Joan returned the compliment by christening her own son John. It is hard to avoid the suspicion that Master John Chaucer had been a teenage troublemaker with an eye to the main chance.

Another Chaucer relation, the widowed Albreda, kept the Holly Tavern, just the other side of Tavern Street. One day in 1338 she had a row with a customer, Roger Bande, possibly about his father's windmill. (He had raised a 20 foot mound on his property and built a windmill on top, overlooking the orchard and vineyard of his neighbour Geoffrey Costyn, who had successfully sued him for damages of

£10.) Whatever it was that Albreda said, young Bande drew his sword and cut off her left hand. The wound killed her, but Bande escaped. Six years later, as a guest at the Priory of Holy Trinity, he met Costyn himself, got into an argument, killed him, and escaped for a second time. Costyn's widow married Geoffrey Stace after Agnes's death.

There is the story of another widow, a contemporary of Albreda, called Maud Allizoun. She lived a couple of miles outside town and one night was attacked by a thief who got away with her four sheep. She tracked him down, catching him red-handed with her animals the following Saturday in Cornhill. She was told that to get him arrested she would have to find two substantial burgesses to vouch for her, which she did. The thief rashly elected for trial by jury and was hanged.

There is the sad tale of Katherine Drinkasoppe, an unmarried mother, who, having baptised her new baby John, broke his neck. She hid his body in a basket under some rubbish and threw the basket onto the Colehill. She herself got off, but John's father, like Maud's thief, was hanged.

Other cases are more humdrum: the wife of a schoolmaster who claimed she had been raped by the Rector of Nacton; the labourer in 1362, when jobs were plentiful after the Black Death, who tried to organise a strike for wages of 3 pence a day plus food; Samuel who was fined a shilling for practising witchcraft (a rare mention of this centuries-old activity); the medical malpractice litigations after promised cures had failed.

Personal weapons were carried as a matter of course. Indeed, during the chronic alarms over invasion or rebellion, it was an offence not to. And, despite the curfew, and the nightwatchmen, and the lanterns in theory outside every door until past midnight (tallow, only obtainable from a duopoly of chandlers, had frequently to be rationed) the streets at night were far from empty.

Eavesdropping after dark under unglazed windows – few could afford glass – required special skills, like blackmail or intimacy with the victim's commercial rival, to maximise its profitability. The less sophisticated, the 'common garrulators', simply did it to cause a nuisance. The usual fine for these people was about twice that for the illegal dung-dumpers.

During the course of the thirteenth century, trial by ordeal of fire or water gave place to trial by jury. We know there was an ordeal pit in Ipswich because its site was sold in 1300. Ipswich jurors were chosen in an extraordinary way: 10 nominees were divided into two groups of

The Crane on the Common Quay.

5, and a dagger (presumably from behind one group) thrown between the two: the 5 towards whom its handle pointed on landing were discharged, as was one, chosen by the accused, out of the remaining 5. This was twice repeated with 20 more men to produce the 12 needed.

It has been suggested a medieval defendant's chances of securing a fair jury trial were about 50/50, probably better odds than the lie-detector technique of the ordeal. Jury service was unpopular, not least because jurors could be sued by the loser in a case. If the verdict went against them, they faced imprisonment.

Prison, otherwise, was less likely for the guilty than a fine, the pillory or the gallows. The prison population was mostly on remand; and since the accused had the right in a jury case, as in the ordeal, to refuse trial, he often did so, and remained where he was. In that way he avoided the risk of being hanged, with the resultant confiscation of his property and his family's ruin. Moreover, life in prison on remand was not intolerable if you could afford it.

After the receipt of the Charter, the town built a jail of its own near Buttermarket. By 1334 it had been moved to the Westgate: in 1448 a second was added a few yards away at the top of Black Horse Lane near the Wolsey Theatre, and a further storey of cells built above the Westgate itself.

The prison service was run on private enterprise lines in the charge of a beadle who had to produce financial sureties against escapes. His salary was only 160 pence a year, but he enjoyed useful fees in addition: 14 pence per head for admissions in the sixteenth century and 40 pence for discharges, plus 6 pence a day for food and 2 pence for lodgings, both paid by the prisoner. He also received one penny every time he swore on oath in Court, but this went towards food for the poorer inmates. Another source of income was the provision of prisoners' extra luxuries, one of which was to be excused from wearing chains.

The pillory in Cornhill was obviously used for a variety of misdemeanours, including cheating at cards. It was a standard punishment for dishonest tradesmen; millers are often mentioned, the notorious short-changers of the middle ages. The penalty for a first offence was typically 2 hours in the pillory, and for the second 8 hours. Another punishment was to hang a placard round the culprit's neck announcing his crime, and drive him round town in or behind a tumbril.

In 1477 a crane was erected on the Common Quay. It had a secondary use to the shifting of cargo. Chiding women could be suspended from it over the Orwell and, if needs be, submerged in a Ducking Stool.

CHAPTER FIVE

The Cardinal

In 1534 an unusual item was on sale among the stalls of the Fishmarket: a little volume entitled *A History of the Gospels*, the earliest surviving book with an Ipswich imprint. Written by an early Christian Spaniard in Latin hexameters, it had been selected some years earlier by Wolsey for use in schools. It was in the Fishmarket because the publisher, Reginald Oliver, lived there. His house adjoined that of the now destitute Whitefriars from whom he was about to purchase several pieces of land for the expansion of his premises.

Gone were the days when it was politely said of the insufferable Father Barmynham that 'there was no subject divine or human on which he could not speak accurately and learnedly'. The religious houses no longer enjoyed such respect, or the cash which went with it. On a corner-post, for example, of a house built around 1490 at the bottom of Foundation Street in the shadow of Blackfriars church, someone had carved a fox in a friar's habit preaching to a congregation of geese; a century earlier that man would have been in trouble. New ideas, spread by the printing presses of men like Oliver were undermining the authority, as well as the self-confidence, of the clergy. Another Whitefriar, John Bale, a distinguished author, left the order about this time to get married, and advised others to do likewise.

Even the Augustinian Canons had got through much of their previous wealth. At St Peter and Paul in 1526 no reliable accounts were being kept, and there was no novice master, perhaps because there were no novices. Its buildings were run down and many of its priests got up too late for Matins, and sometimes apparently for lunch. At Holy Trinity they were failing to keep the proper silences, and came and went as they pleased without asking the Prior's permission. Their servants were insolent, and the cook incompetent and dirty.

It was probably a joint initiative of the Priories and the Merchants' Guild which founded the boys' grammar school at some date before 1400. The schoolmasters were sometimes laymen and sometimes

Friar Fox and his congregation of geese.

priests, at least one of whom doubled up as chaplain to the Guild. Richard Penyngton, a layman, is the first recorded master. After his retirement he beat up a butcher and had to be restrained by the Court from interfering in the school's affairs.

School fees were 8 pence a quarter and, as a going rate for a schoolmaster's pay was around £10 a year (£5,000 in today's currency) it is possible that from the beginning he had a minimum of 40 pupils. Sir Thomas More claimed that over half the male population of England was literate by 1500, and (even if he was too optimistic) it is not unreasonable to assume that among the 200 wealthiest households of Ipswich a century earlier, there might have been 40 boys at any one time to fill its school. Also, there were no doubt a few boarders from out of town. For that they would have paid an extra £2 a year, plus keep.

Apart from the infants – the Apes' Eyes – taught their ABC[1] by someone else, there were three grades of pupils spread over eight years, primary, secondary and 'grammar' (the top three classes) whose aim was to acquire a final fluency in Latin and the rudiments of logic.

The school's original site is nowhere mentioned, and all the teaching may have taken place in a church. However, in 1483, Richard Felaw, a former Bailiff whose only daughter had married a Fastolf, left his substantial property in Foundation Street to be used as a school, with a house adjoining for the master. He also provided a legacy to give a free education to a dozen or more boys whose parents had land worth less than £1 a year or stock-in-trade worth less than £20. There was another condition: they must attend daily sung Mass at Blackfriars at 6am.

Whatever sanitary arrangements had been in use previously at Felaw's house, they proved inadequate for a school, although it took several years to find out. Then a strip of land was leased from the town to erect a privy across the road up against the Blackfriars' wall. The rent was a red rose. Felaw, like many townspeople, had been loyal to the White Rose of York; but Felaw was dead, while Henry VII with his Red Rose was still very much alive, and had twice visited Ipswich within months of seizing power.

Thomas Wolsey was probably in his third or fourth year at school at the time of Felaw's death. An only child, his parents had moved to Ipswich from the Stowmarket area some years before he was born. His father, Robert, was not well off, but the family had rich relations in

1. B was pronounced like P, and C more like sigh', hence Apes' Eyes.

Ipswich – notably the Daundys – whom they may have expected to help them. Perhaps they did, like paying for Thomas's schooling, but Robert, an innkeeper and then a butcher, seems to have been his own worst enemy, often in Court for stupid, petty offences, such as keeping a brothel, letting his pigs run wild, selling short measures of ale or bad meat pies, and so on. Just before or after Thomas's birth, he bought a small house in St Nicholas's parish for £8, so he was by no means penniless. Even so, he never bothered to become an Ipswich freeman, an obvious investment for anyone like him, and with his connections, surely simple to arrange. It looks as if young Thomas may have inherited his brains from mother.

Robert died in 1496, leaving £2 for a mural of St Michael in St Nicholas's north aisle, fragments of which have been uncovered. He had become a churchwarden in 1491, perhaps influenced by the fact that his son was training at Oxford for the priesthood.

For 400 years ambitious young men, like their Victorian descendants, had looked to service in the Crown's overseas possessions as a quick way to advancement. There was little left now except the enclave of Calais, and in 1502 Thomas obtained the post of chaplain to

Ruins of St. Peter and Paul Priory, photographed in the 19th. Century.

its deputy lieutenant. A minor job, but it served its purpose: by 1515 he was a Cardinal.

The red hat was hardly broken in before he obtained royal and papal permission to reform the monasteries, in other words to close down the richest and most vulnerable, and use their money for a great scholastic combine; and just as in the case of Winchester with New College, Oxford, and of Eton with King's, Cambridge, so St Mary's, Ipswich, would become the feeder school for his Cardinal College at Oxford.

His original idea was to build the school on a green-field site beyond the Westgate, probable incorporating the chapel of Our Lady of Ipswich, whose miraculous powers had been further demonstrated in the very year he became Cardinal. A school with a miracle-working chapel would undoubtedly have appealed to his considerable vanity, and even encouraged recruitment. Raising the cash, however, may have been more difficult than he had imagined. The plums had been picked two generations earlier by Henry VI for Eton and King's, and feeling against his widespread closures – 200 in all – was strong. Henry VIII twice warned him in shrewd letters which anyhow could not be ignored, of the 'many that mumble' behind his back.

The priory of St Peter and Paul, with its church and other buildings already in place, looked better value, so he took over that. And, being near the quay, the importation of bricks and stone was cheaper. There was a useful outcrop of stone offshore at Harwich, but to his fury it turned out to be essential as a breakwater (it was quarried with disastrous consequences by the Victorians) and his cousin, Robert Daundy, had to bring in more costly material from a quarry in Normandy.

Much new building was necessary. As well as 50 boarding 'foundation scholars', St Mary's was to include all the grammar school pupils plus a Dean, 2 masters, 12 male and 6 boy choristers, and 8 lay brothers. Moreover, the Cardinal's prestige had roused the educational aspirations of the whole region: 'the flock hourly increases', he was told after the school had been open for 3 months, 'so that the house is too small'.

The headmaster's salary was an exceptionally generous £24 a year. The male choristers, who were priests (one likes to think re-employed Canons from the priory) were less happy and soon went on strike for better pay and breakfasts. The breakfasts were improved but not the pay.

The foundation stone was laid in June 1528. School started 3 months later, evidently among the 37 stone masons and all their construction work. It is possible that the new boarders were housed in the old priory buildings, while school continued as before in Felaw's house.

For two years before moving to Calais, Wolsey had been headmaster of Magdalen College School in Oxford, and he was genuinely interested in education. His own eminent hand had set out the national curriculum. Apart from a sound belief in a good grounding of grammar, his views are distinctly modern. Lessons must be interesting, with a strong emphasis in the early years on Latin conversation. Even for the rowdier 11-plus age groups he warns against the temptation of beating knowledge into the boys. The top form should be taught to

Wolsey (left) discusses the building of St. Mary's School with Thomas Cromwell and an unknown bishop.

Wolsey's Gate in the 18th. Century.

write English properly, rather than spend so much time on logic. And learning by heart, he says, is best done at the end of the day.

September 8th was the feast of the Nativity of Our Lady, and the Cardinal ordered that there should be an annual procession on that day from the school to Her shrine in Lady Lane. Ominously, the weather was so bad in 1528 that it had to be cancelled. Wolsey himself was not able to be present (he had also been absent from the stone-laying ceremony) but many local dignitaries turned up, as well as the Cardinal's sinister assistant Thomas Cromwell. They processed round St Peter's, heard Mass, and sat down to the usual feast, a bottle party provided by the guests.

A year later the builders were still there, preparing to knock down for reuse the stones they had just put up. There was no point in demolishing the brickwork, and they left for posterity the boundary wall (or part of it) and a side entrance now called Wolsey's gate. Commissioners arrived to compute and confiscate the school's massive endowment producing an income of over £2,500 a year. Wolsey had fallen; and some months later the King formally dissolved St Mary's. Its sister foundation at Oxford was just finished and, with its name changed to Christ Church, was reprieved.

Ipswich grammar school, now under royal patronage, was allowed to retain £50 a year from the Cardinal's foundation by way of a reduction in the town's land tax (the old geld) due to the Crown. The headmaster's salary remained at £24, and the second master was kept on. No doubt he was needed if many of St Mary's new boys remained in school. Someone looked up the old minutes of the Great Court agreeing to the amalgamation of the grammar school with St Mary's, and added a brief scrawl in the margin that the arrangement was void.

St Mary's one and only headmaster did not long survive the Cardinal's downfall. The appointment for the next 40 years, until Queen Elizabeth's common sense restored it to the Bailiffs and the Bishop of Norwich, was in the hands of a shambolic Crown office in Whitehall which took a minimal interest in the school, got into a muddle over its payments, and after long delays produced a series of unsupervised idlers to head it.

For much of the time the school must have been held together by an energetic doctor of medicine, an expert on necromancy and oriental studies, called Richard Argentine who became second master in 1537. He was an ardent Protestant, but his wife conveniently died before Bloody Mary came to the throne, and so, covering Ipswich was graffiti proclaiming his loyalty to her, he switched back to Rome and took Holy Orders. His reward was the headmastership of Ipswich School of life. Under Elizabeth, having given up the school, he enjoyed a second career as a Protestant pluralist with the livings of St Clement's and St Helen's, plus several more in other parts of the country.

St Peter's church was returned to its former parishioners, and Thomas Alvard, an Ipswich agent of Wolsey, and then a spy of Cromwell, was given the six derelict acres of the old priory, together with the job of shipping the stones and other reusable material to London. Some disappeared into local buildings, including the foundation stone, rediscovered in the eighteenth century, and now at Christ Church, Oxford.

CHAPTER SIX

Henry Tooley

'I WARN YOU that you do put away all your workfolks', wrote Henry Tooley to his wife Alice in 1543, 'both joiners and masons ... for I will be no longer troubled with them'. His patience had snapped and, like many another, he wanted to see the back of builders messing about indefinitely at his home. It is the only surviving letter from this stubborn and formidable old man, the richest merchant in Ipswich.

He has achieved fame not so much because of the commercial successes of his life, or the generosity of the benefactions after his death, but because of the years thereafter when his executors were disentangling his accounts. For this reason they were carefully preserved, and now provide a unique insight into one of the largest enterprises of the period outside London.

Tooley made up his accounts personally, but he was an untidy man, none too numerate, and had no truck with the sophistication of double-entry book-keeping. And, like most merchants, he still used Roman, rather than Arabic, numerals, which cannot have made for clarity. At his death he was owed at least £2,000 from over 160 different sources, about half in value going back over 17 years, and these of course were the main cause of his executors' protracted headaches.

Including the debts, he seems to have left nearly £5,000. That is under £1m today, and not an enormous sum by the contemporary standards of the landed gentry: in 1523, when Tooley had the eleventh highest tax bill in Ipswich, the Duke of Norfolk's had been 40 times higher.

The Tooleys lived in Key Street immediately to the west of the Common Quay with a separate walled garden a hundred yards away at its other end. The house had a 74 foot frontage on the quay and was built round a central courtyard. Onto this gave the bay window of a large parlour with an interior glazed gallery above. Another parlour overlooked the quay. Tooley's office, a big room probably with

The Tooley's house from the Common Quay.

several tables, and certainly with scales, an abacus and a locked chest or safe, was most likely near the front door on Key Street. Some rooms, and of course the cellars, were used for storing merchandise. He had other warehouses scattered round the town, including one at his mother-in-law's house nearby in St Clement's.

He and Alice had had three children, John and two girls, but they had all died in childhood or adolescence. Henry's apprentices, several at any one time, who under their articles had to live with him, may have been a solace or an extra burden after their bereavements. During most of the apprentices' 7 years of service, they worked at Key Street, relieved by occasional errands into the country, and finishing at last with spells at Tooley's agencies overseas.

Alice was that unusual phenomenon of the period, an educated woman. Apart from running the home and coping with the apprentices – aged 16 upwards – she took an active part in her husband's business and was in charge during his frequent absences abroad. She seems to have been much younger than him, perhaps by 20 years.

Tooley first appears as a householder in Ipswich in 1499, probably in his mid-20's. The earliest recorded transactions for his own account start in 1515, importing woad and a couple of barrels of wine from Bordeaux. The following year it was 51 barrels from Bordeaux and goods with a wholesale value of £185 from Antwerp, including 4 cwt of cotton wool, 6 tons of black soap, 2 tons of woad and a bundle of fans.

In 1520 he appointed Simon Cowper, a London tailor, as his agent in Bordeaux and Bilbao. After 18 months Cowper reported back in person to Key Street. He had barely tethered his horse before he was set upon by Tooley who impounded his baggage and marched him off to jail. There he remained without money for 10 months, Tooley having hung onto his £4 of cash as well as the horse which he sold for £7. The affair dragged on in the Courts for years. Tooley claimed he

Henry Tooley, from his brass (the screw through his cheek is a piece of recent vandalism).

had been robbed, but exactly how is unclear: certainly Cowper's expenses were in dispute and possibly there were problems over his purchase of the *Mary Walsingham* for £152, Tooley's first and only ship. Or Cowper may simply have been incompetent, and dealt at bad prices.

An identical fate soon befell another agent called Spar after Tooley had bumped into him by chance in the street. That case, too, ran for years. Spar seems to have been negligent rather than dishonest, but the effect was the same on Tooley.

Bordeaux wines in those days, both red and white, reached their peak after about four months, and seldom kept beyond a year. A poor vintage or, as in 1521, the threat of war, could therefore produce sharp price movements. In that year, when many merchants were reluctant to risk their ships, Tooley imported thirty barrels of wine at a probable cost of about £3 each. After combined freight and duty charges of £1, they would normally have retailed for about £5 a barrel (around 150 gallons) giving him a profit of some £30 for the whole shipment. But the retail price had doubled, so his profit this time was £180, or about £50,000 today. It looks like the break he had been waiting for.

Tooley rented a house and cellars in Bordeaux, and often visited the city both for the October vintage and again in February. The wine of course had to be tasted, an important matter which could not be left entirely to agents – and certainly not to apprentices, although one can imagine jolly evenings at Key Street while they learnt the art.

Tooley balanced his imports with what was virtually the town's only export, Suffolk cloth. Most of this, produced locally but by no means all from local sheep, he purchased undyed (either on credit or exchanging for woad) where the foreign market was both larger and unencumbered by the frivolities of fashion, a growing menace with which the dyers of Ipswich proved ill-equipped to deal.

Wine was a winter trade. In summer the *Mary Walsingham* imported French salt or woad, or was chartered out to a seamen's co-operative for the Icelandic fisheries. Tooley's charge for this was £90 for the 5 months' season plus a proportion of the catch. He also sold them the salt, hooks and lines and other items. His accounts show that in 1532 the share of 'myself, Harry Tooley' was 20 per cent and earned him £160; in 1534 it was just £62.

The *Mary Walsingham* was not a large ship, under 100 tons, with a capacity for at least 66 barrels of wine or salted cod. For the Bordeaux voyage – 2 weeks each way and several ashore – the Master received £4 and the dozen crew members 18 shillings each or less, half paid on reaching France so that they could trade a bit on their own account and/or spend a few nights on the town. Although they were mostly Suffolk men, not many names are recorded for more than one trip.

The river at the Common Quay at this period was often too shallow for vessels over 30 tons. (The old tide mill at Stoke Bridge, recently taken over by a fuller for washing cloth, was thought to be the culprit but the cause of the silting-up was more fundamental and nothing was done about it.) On these occasions the *Mary Walsingham's* cargo had to be transhipped onto or from local hoys a couple of miles downstream near the old Roman ford by today's Orwell Bridge. After unloading from an Iceland trip she was said to 'stink so that no man not used to the same can endure it'. Strong words for those days, but it never seems to have harmed the wine.

By 1543, Tooley was nearly 70. Winter journeys to Bordeaux must have become ever more burdensome, and his wine dealings – 103 barrels in 1538 – had trickled to a standstill. The *Mary Walsingham* was sold, scrapped or sunk: he spent £20 on a hulk as a replacement for her but soon got rid of it.

Antwerp, where probably since the days of his own apprenticeship, he had always been an active dealer, was nearer and more cosmopolitan; and with its immense range of merchandise, an ideal market for an old man to dabble in: nails and scythes, madder and woad, silks, spices, sugar lumps and straw hats, hops, alum, playing cards and tennis balls, not to mention cloth in all the latest colours. One of his cargoes contained a consignment of books for Oliver's shop in the Fishmarket, but most of his trade now was into and out of London.

In 1521, at the crucial stage of his career, a possibly jealous Bailiff had forced on him the financial appointment of chamberlain. He turned it down and was fined £4: changing his mind, he took up the job, changed his mind again, and was fined again; but he got out of it. Another fine of £40 for some unknown transgression he refused to pay, and was deprived of the freedom of the town. He responded by switching his operations to Yarmouth, and 18 months later it was restored for nothing.

Tooley's closest friend was Robert Daundy, Wolsey's cousin and son of the merchant Edmund Daundy, builder of the town cross which for 300 years occupied the centre of Cornhill. Rebuilt or repaired several times, and possibly much altered, it survives in sketches as an open pillared octagon, 27 feet across, supporting a dome crowned by a Maltese cross. Balanced on top of that, a later addition, stood a figure of Justice with her usual trappings.

Daundy senior left over £1,000 in 1525, about half Tooley's probable £5,000 estate, adjusting for the intervening 26 years of inflation. Prices rose 5-fold in the century between 1510 and 1610 while wages only doubled; and the new men, tough, bucaneering, middle class, who had acquired the monastic estates at the Reformation, were disinclined to spend time or money, as their pious predecessors had done, on daily handouts to the growing number of paupers at their gates.

Edmund Withypoll, the gentrified heir to a large fortune of Bristol merchants, bought Holy Trinity Priory and its 650 acres in 1544 for £2,000. He moved to Ipswich from Walthamstow (where – under his original name of Vediopolo in the official record – he had obtained a royal pardon for the murder of a local yeoman) and on the site of the old priory built himself a mansion – today's museum – which he called Christchurch Withypoll. Thereafter he began a series of battles with the town authorities: an unsuccessful effort to incorporate St Margaret's churchyard into his domain; a dispute over a bridleway; an argument over fishing rights; an absurd attempt to restore his manorial jurisdiction over Holyrood Fair, the big September market held for centuries in St Margaret's Green. Not surprisingly, he never became a freeman.

It was the town's golden age, and inside the ramparts too not only were the rich building many fine houses, but as wealth trickled down the economic scale, the less well-off were active also. Lacking great public buildings, this was the glory of Ipswich: the uncontrived harmony of the whole central area, street after street of good houses, large and small, put up by confident people determined to display and enjoy their new prosperity; houses to last, which their children and grandchildren would be proud of, with pleasant gardens and many trees. Today, after two hundred years of industrial exploitation, architectural mistakes and planning intrasingence, little remains.

The Ancient House in Buttermarket survives as a famous exception: built by Thomas Fastolf of Nacton – grandson of Shakespeare's Falstaff - and extended by a London draper and fishmonger, George Copping, it was at length purchased by the Sparrows. They had the Fishmarket moved eastwards (demand had plummeted since the Reformation) and turned the house into outwardly the grandest grocer's shop in Europe.

Other houses were put up by the local gentry for their occasional visits to the town. Sir Robert Curson (Withypoll's grandfather) had one at the corner of Silent Street and Rose Lane, and Sir Anthony

The Seckfords' palace in Westgate Street.

Wingfield, Henry VIII's friend and executor, in Tacket Street. Although elaborately decorated, neither was especially large: the great parlour in Curson's house measured 33 feet by 22, and Wingfield's 27 by 17. The King's brother-in-law, the Duke of Suffolk, had a house in Brook Street, and the Seckfords of Bealings a flamboyant little palace where today's Museum Street joins Westgate Street.

Like the Tooleys, the richest merchants lived near the river. The Percyvales' address was The Longhouse and the Sabyns' The Steelyard. Richard Percyvale spent much of his time copying out and updating Le Domesday, concluding with the addition of several pages of doggerel, not of his own composition, about the Kings of England. William Sabyn, owner and Master of *The Sabyn*, who bought Blackfriars from the Crown for £24, combined commerce with piracy and fighting the French. One Danish victim, laden with rye, he brought back to Ipswich; his main regret on that occasion was his lack of resources to burn half a dozen villages on the way home. Nearby in Fore Street lived Thomas Eldred, a tallow chandler. His son in 1586 enlisted under the squire of Trimley, Thomas Cavendish, in the first expedition after Drake's to circumnavigate the globe.

Thomas Pownder, another quayside resident, is now remembered less for his worldly success than for the fine brass over his grave in St Mary Quay. And Robert Wymbull would be quite forgotten but for his brass in St Mary le Tower and the chance of his having fined Wolsey's father for selling those bad meat pies; while the memorial on a wall at the back of the same church to the draper William Smart, unwitting founder, among other charities, of the Town Library, is chiefly of interest for its view of Ipswich in 1600.

Tooley died in 1551, leaving the bulk of his fortune to a charitable foundation whose main purpose was to provide almshouses for 10 ex-servicemen. They were also to receive clothes (a livery incorporating Tooley's red and blue colours) firewood and medical care, together with 6 pence a week, and more for those who couldn't work, provided they attended morning and evening service at St Mary Quay.

Alice and his sister, Joan, tried to upset the will, and there was trouble with dishonest executors so it was eleven years before 5 almshouses, either for husband and wife or for two men sharing, each surrounded by its own garden, were ready for occupation. They were probably in the half-acre orchard off Star Lane which he and Alice had leased from the Blackfriars in the 1530's.

The peace of this gentle retreat was soon endangered by developments nearby. In order to deal with rising poverty, the town acquired the Blackfriars premises from Sabyn's successor and set up Christ's Hospital in a southern portion of its ample buildings. Neither Christian nor a hospital (the friars' church was demolished) it became a workhouse for 40 inmates, both deserving and undeserving poor of both sexes and all ages. Someone called it a 'seminary of thieves'. Vagrants were rounded up and sent there as a punishment for a limited period, but within a generation, children predominated.

To pay for all this, a poor rate was raised of £170 a year, a penny or twopence a week from most of the 312 taxable householders (the richest, Edmund Withypoll, paid 16 pence) half of which went towards running Christ's Hospital, and half as 'outdoor' relief to around 80 impoverished families in their own homes – actors, witches, and rabbit-skin salesmen specifically excepted. That was in the 1570's; by 1597 there were nearly twice as many on outdoor relief, and extra funds were conveniently made available by Tooley's trustees who were also town officials.

An incomplete census of the poor for that year mentions 400 men, women and children from 9 parishes, 80 per cent being in St Matthew's and St Clement's in the suburbs, and St Nicholas's in the town. The actual total, including the 3 unrecorded parishes plus Christ's Hospital and Tooley's and Daundy's almshouses (the latter founded by Edmund Daundy in Lady Lane) would have been nearer 600. This is comparable to the figure in 1297 at the time of the wedding of Edward I's daughter, Princess Elizabeth, when, despite the many intervening plagues, the population as a whole is likely to have been smaller.

There were two further outbreaks of plague about this time, in 1579 and 1585, and the town's by now well-oiled machinery rolled into action. 'Viewers' were employed to report victims' names and addresses, nurses recruited to help them, and special watchmen taken on to control and isolate infected areas. Free food, candles, wood and medicine were supplied to the sick, and extra cash – 18 pence a week for the elderly and a shilling for the young – handed out to those compulsorily evacuated. Cats and dogs were destroyed in designated streets. Bonfires everywhere were kept alight, not to burn the deceaseds' clothes and bedding which were buried in their back gardens, but as a general fumigation of Ipswich air.

By 1600, Christ's Hospital and the almshouses of the Tooley Foundation, though separately managed and set up with rather different intentions, were moving towards an ever-closer union. And the road running beside the Blackfriars western wall soon acquired its present name of Foundation Street.

CHAPTER SEVEN

The Road to Agawam

QUEEN ELIZABETH visited Ipswich in July 1561: two weeks later her cousin, Catherine Seymour, eight months pregnant, was sent to the Tower of London. Tradition, not wholly to be ignored in such matters, has it that the two events are linked. Catherine's grandmother was Princess Mary, the Duchess of Suffolk, Henry VIII's sister who had a town house in Brook Street.

Catherine's father and eldest sister, Lady Jane Grey, the nine-days queen, had been beheaded by Queen Mary seven years earlier. Within days, her mother had got remarried to a common groom (the description is Queen Elizabeth's) of exactly her daughter's age. Catherine, 'the Lady of Lamentation, seldom seen with dry eyes', died under house arrest at Yoxford in 1567.

Such is the circumstantial evidence which connects Ipswich with the Grey sisters. And it may be significant that it was at Ipswich that Queen Mary had first received confirmation from the Secretary of State, William Cecil, of her own acceptance as queen when she arrived in the town with all her supporters from Framlingham in 1553.

In the chaotic years of Henry VIII's break with Rome, Mary's reunion and the Elizabethan settlement, Ipswich – after London and Bristol and largest Puritan centre in England – achieved a political importance never enjoyed before or since: a trend-setter, nearer the continent than Bristol, less diverse than London, more exposed than either to the new ideas from Lutheran Europe.

The seed has been sown in the 1350's by Philippa of Hainault, Edward III's queen, who first suggested her compatriot Dutch cloth-workers should be encouraged to settle in East Anglia. It was they who dragged Ipswich into the fifteenth century, adding value to its wool exports by converting them far more lucratively into cloth, and circumventing in the process the cramping restrictive practices of hostmen and the like; producing, as is the way of capitalism initially, greater riches for the already rich, another cause of dissatisfaction with the old religion.

Swollen by religious refugees, bearers of potent witness to both God and Mammon, the town's Dutch colony by 1485 was several hundred strong. Over 30 Dutch surnames are recorded at this time, and there must have been plenty of others, like the publisher Reginald Oliver, Dr Argentine the schoolmaster and William Sabyn the merchant, who had prudently anglicised theirs.

They soon diversified into more profitable trades than weaving, setting up as coopers, hatters, cobblers and brickmakers, as well as brewers of a new beer made from hops, a Dutch export. Much of the elaborate carving on the beams and corner-posts of the opulent new houses springing up all over town was their work.

Some became merchants, trading with Antwerp where their antecedents gave them a clear advantage. There was a good deal of grumbling in Ipswich over that, as over their natural preference for employing their own countrymen rather than locals. Although there was no ghetto-like Dutch quarter, they tended to congregate near the river. They established their own church somewhere in that area and for a time after the Reformation rented bits of the old Blackfriars' buildings from William Sabyn as warehouses. They were a restless lot, coming and going all over East Anglia, and seldom settling in one place for more than a couple of generations; but their residence was of immense benefit to Ipswich, and Queen Philippa has seldom received due credit for her initiative.

Hell, rightly or wrongly, is of less concern to us than it was to our ancestors who viewed heresy in much the same way as we regard drug-addiction. Henry VIII's divorce gave a political twist to this ancient menace. London vied with Rome in the publication of new heresies, new crimes, created, it must have seemed to many, at the whim of authority, and varying subtly with each change of monarch. The punishment too, burning at the stake, was far removed from the swift, familiar operation of the gallows. The mood of the crowd, the 2,000 or more that filled Cornhill at these conflagrations, gleeful or sombre, laughing and weeping, always emotional, sometimes inspired, is impossible to imagine.

Heretics were normally burnt between 7 o'clock and 10 o'clock in the morning, chained to a sixpenny stake by the meat market in front of the Shambles in the south-east corner of Cornhill. It was probably

The Tudor Shambles.

the very spot used for bull-baiting between the two trees that stand today outside the old Post Office.

Officials sat in the Shambles gallery, whence a clergyman, once the faggots and brushwood had been piled up, would deliver an appropriate sermon. Then the condemned man or woman was permitted a final speech, which might take some time. 'On, on', shouted a Bailiff on one occasion, 'have done, have done', and the brushwood was duly set alight. Once Sir Robert Curson got so excited that he came down from the gallery, cut a branch with his sword off a tree nearby, and added it to the flames.

These grim spectacles were not frequent. Details of only two are recorded under Henry VIII and three under Mary. One of the latter concerned the fate of the popular Parson of East Bergholt, Richard Samuel. Being a married man, he had had to surrender his now Catholic parish, but he remained in the village to help. His wife returned to Ipswich where, refusing to give her up, he was arrested on one of his nocturnal visits. The jailer at the Westgate was a known Protestant sympathiser, so Samuel was soon dispatched to Norwich, being at length brought back to the stake at Ipswich, a physical wreck.

Agnes Wardall's experience was rather different. The egregious Dr Argentine, now a Catholic priest and headmaster of the grammar school, having discovered she was still a practising Protestant, took some soldiers one night to arrest her at her home in St Clement's. She was a heavy sleeper, and her maid had a job to wake her up, locking her just in time into a tiny cupboard. 'This is a fair cupboard', said one of the soldiers, but he never tried to open it. By the time they left, Agnes was gasping for air; but the key was mislaid and, when discovered, jammed in the lock. Prayer was their last resort, but it worked.

Her friend and neighbour, another devout Protestant, was the widowed Alice Tooley, viciously described by an old Catholic customer of her husband as 'swelled by too much riches into wealth'. No doubt she would have heard Agnes's story at some length the next morning, and that may have persuaded her to retire temporarily to the relative obscurity of Darsham.

One of the last executions to take place on Cornhill was that of John Robinson, an elderly Catholic priest from Yorkshire who was hanged, drawn and quartered in 1585.

The Reformation whitewashed the interiors of the town's churches, stripped them of their roods and screens, and confiscated their treasures. Much of their stained glass was smashed, definitely nine windows in St Lawrence's. The desecration was so thorough that 100 years later little remained for the notorious wrecker, William Dowsing, and his men: the rest of the stained glass, 10 brasses and 16 crosses, hard to reach; a brace of angels at St Mary Stoke, 3 more at St Matthew's plus the 12 stone apostles at St Margaret's, and that was all.

The churches' tithes had been sold or granted to new lay patrons who proved unsurprisingly reluctant to share them with incumbent clergy of whatever persuasion. At one stage in Mary's reign, only two churches had priests. Even the Bishop's palace in Holywell's Park, the royal Domesday estate given to the diocese by Richard I, had gone back to the Crown.

The hated Hopton, Mary's Dominican Bishop of Norwich – Ipswich was in his diocese – conveniently died within a month of the Queen herself. The new man, John Parkhurst, was a distinguished Puritan, and he was able to turn Sir Robert Curson's former house in Silent Street into his Ipswich palace.

Bishop Parkhurst reorganised the parochial finances and gave a more structured Protestant veneer to Puritan worship. The clergy were encouraged to wear the surplice again, and the faithful, under pain of imprisonment, to dress more soberly. The current extravagant fashions from Venice, Paris and Antwerp, where a pair of padded breeches could cost the modern equivalent of £1,000, were considered socially divisive, a drain on the balance of payments, and displeasing to the Almighty.

In 1577 the post of Town Preacher, previously almost a sinecure involving no more than a quarterly uplifting address, was redesignated. In exchange for £50 a year, good long sermons every Sunday, Wednesday and Friday were now demanded before the Town Council in St Mary le Tower. Such exposure to such a congregation, Puritan to a man and well aware of who controlled the purse strings, needed a preacher of quite special talents. Ten were tried, before in 1605 they got the right one.

St. Mary le Tower, before the 19th. Century restoration.

This was Samuel Ward who remained in the job until his death 34 years later, with two intermissions in a London prison: the first for drawing and publishing a skilful caricature of the King of Spain in close consultation with the devil, the second for describing the religion of the Church of England as, among other things, 'stood on tiptoes, ready to be gone'. But a great preacher requires more than the ability to turn a phrase, and it is in his portrait rather than in his published sermons (their title pages decorated by himself) that the power of his charm, humour and sincerity can be seen most clearly. During his second term of imprisonment, 'a little leisure occasioned against my will', the Bishop tried to remove him, but Ipswich would have none of it; and so, after a few days of rioting, he remained.

William Smart's library, 12 years after his death was still in crates in the vestry of St Mary le Tower, his beneficiary. Ward persuaded the town to set it up as the nucleus of a Town Library for the particular use of himself as Town Preacher, and the northern half of the old Blackfriars dormitory along Lower Orwell Street was furnished to receive it. The rest of the dormitory was divided up, partly as a gunpowder and armaments store and partly as a Hall for the Cloth-workers' Company. Ward's own house was a few minutes walk away in Lower Brook Street. It had been bought for his occupancy in 1609 for £120; 29 years later he was allowed to purchase it from the Corporation for £140, a nice measure of current inflation. He died a rich man, his salary of £120 a year – raised from an initial £67 – regularly augmented by legacies from admirers.

In 1629, the Massachusetts Bay Company was formed largely with Ipswich capital, and with a Suffolk landowner, John Winthrop, as governor. Its purpose was to follow in the wake of the Pilgrim Fathers and found Puritan colonies in the brave New World; the Church of England, in fact, 'ready to be gone'. Eleven ships were chartered and 800 potential emigrants discreetly recruited. Nearly half were from Suffolk. The cost was £5 per head (plus £4 per ton for luggage) but easy terms could be arranged on the basis of sail now, pay – in labour – later. Discretion was necessary because permission was required to leave the country and not always forthcoming if applicants were suspected of fleeing creditors or criminal justice, which they often were. It was easier, especially in Ipswich, simply to pretend you wanted to visit Holland.

Less than 600 people survived the 10 weeks voyage and the first few days on land. Scurvy was the killer for which their remedies were beer and a noisome infusion made from saltpetre, grated nutmeg and a type of cress called scurvy grass. Passengers did their own cooking and stowed their own baggage on deck, sometimes so badly that it was lost overboard. Among it all, when the weather permitted, the men did musketry drill.

By 1634, 40 or more ships had gone over, including the *Patient Endeavour* and the *Elizabeth and Francis* from Ipswich, both just 100 tons. A passenger on the latter was the Rev Nathaniel Ward, Samuel's younger brother, who joined a small group being settled by Winthrop at a place the Indians knew as Agawam. They built a Meeting House there and incorporated themselves into a town, which they called Ipswich.

CHAPTER EIGHT

The Golden Fleece

MEANWHILE in Ipswich, Suffolk, a terminal crisis had overtaken the town's vast export trade, its golden fleece.

By 1530, the cloth industry was mature: the clothiers controlled its manufacture and the merchants its marketing. The latter were mainly organised into local branches of one or other of the two international monopolies, the London Merchant Adventurers, trading into Antwerp, and the Baltic Hanseatic League, headed respectively at that time in Ipswich by Henry Tooley and his piratical neighbour, William Sabyn. Membership was expensive, and the smaller merchants belonged to neither. They prospered because profits were high and the fines, if they were caught, were not large enough to deter them.

The main competition to the Ipswich branch of the Merchant Adventurers was from their colleagues in London, and in 1590 the town's leading clothiers were persuaded to establish a Clothworkers' Company in which all aspects of the trade were represented. Its aim was to share financial and technical information, control wages and enforce standards; a trade federation against the Londoners.

It was soon apparent that this was not the answer. Its managers, having spent a great deal of money setting up their systems, proved too inflexible in their practical application. Nothing but bickering resulted and, if the merchants are to be believed, poorer quality cloth. In particular, even before the government Scheme of 1614, they began to give way to the vested interests of the dyers and finishers on whom, as it was maintained in highly suspect statistics, up to 15,000 Suffolk jobs depended.

Dyeing was an expensive process, and the dyers, sandwiched between the clothiers and the merchants, had remained independent. They were too rich for the former to absorb and too unsophisticated in their techniques, compared with their continental rivals, for the latter to bother with. Much cloth was exported undyed, even from Ipswich where the dyers were unusually strong. This had been illegal for years, but the 1614 Scheme (a monopoly arrangement devised by the London dyers) closed the loopholes. Dutch buyers, deprived of undyed English cloth, turned to other suppliers. Numerous merchants in Ipswich were swiftly bankrupted, and the domino effect ruined the clothiers likewise. In 1622 many had 2 years unsold stock on their hands.

That same year matters came to a head with the London Eastland Company whose customers were less able, or less inclined, than the Dutch to switch suppliers. The company, formed to take over the Baltic monopoly after the English end of the Hanseatic League was closed down in 1578, had a small branch in Ipswich, but local membership was not encouraged.

Four of its London brethren arrived in the town to place their

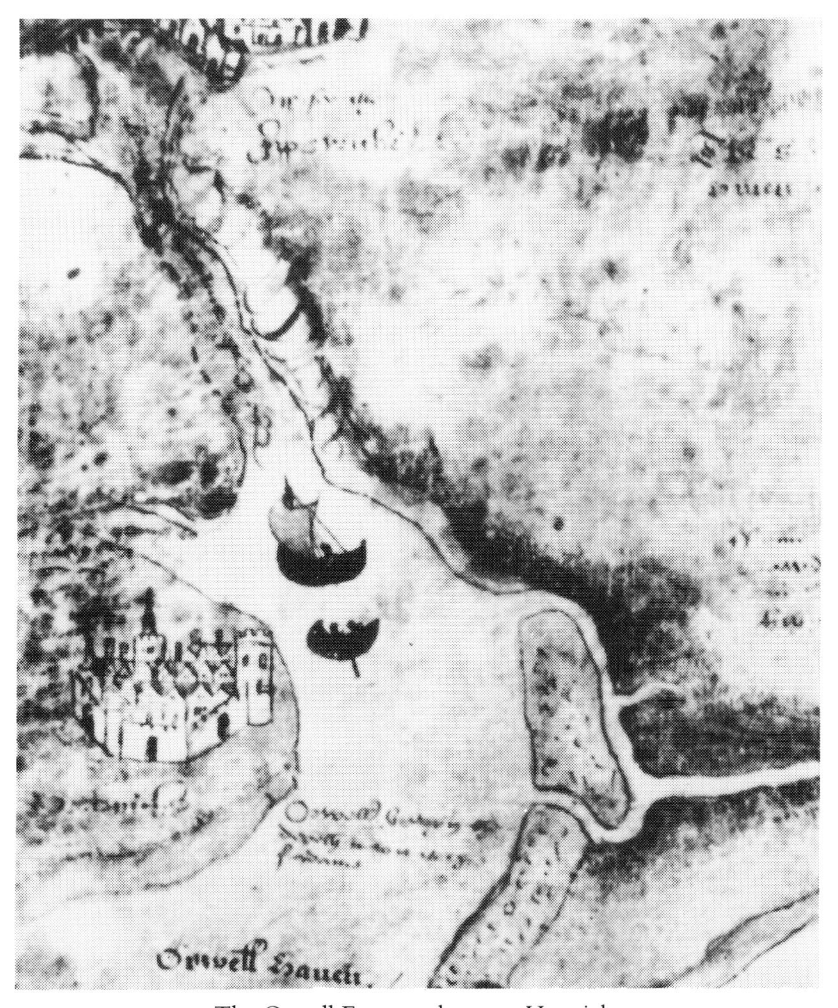

The Orwell Estuary, down to Harwich.

orders for the season. They were quoted prices – this is the Ipswich version – 12 per cent below what they had paid elsewhere. The Londoners demanded further reductions of up to 20 per cent, which they said were the going rates. The clothiers, thinking – correctly – that they themselves could obtain a temporary export licence on hardship grounds, were adamant, and no business resulted. And within 5 years, partly as a result of war and sterling's appreciation, sales to the Eastland Company were down 80 per cent.

The writing had been on the wall for some time. The merchants of London, which was now larger than the 50 largest provincial centres put together, were too powerful and too close. They had better information and wider horizons.

Moreover, two generations earlier, one big opportunity the Ipswich merchants, basking in the evening sunshine of their great prosperity, had totally missed. Suffolk wool had always been of poor quality, and much of the cloth exported from Ipswich, coarse and heavy, was most suitable for country wear. But habits were changing. Lighter and cheaper fabrics were in vogue, Dutch innovations, which were being manufactured in growing quantities, from the same wool differently spun, in and around Sudbury and Colchester, 'slight and vain commodities wherein the common people delight'. But the customer is always right; the London merchants quickly realised the future belonged to these new draperies and once in the market they were unbeatable. If Tooley had been born 50 years later, the subsequent history of Ipswich might have been very different.

Ipswich was left with Russia and Turkish eastern Europe for whose cold winters its products were ideally suited. This was a small but very profitable market because the cloth for it was stretched, a dishonest practice long permitted at Ipswich on the grounds that if it was not done here, the Dutch would do it at Antwerp and reap the benefit.

The industry's fate was not wholly ignored by the government. In 1639 it looked as if the cloth-workers of the whole area might emigrate *en masse* to Holland taking the remains of their industry with them, provided they could ensure supplies of fullers' earth. This came primarily from Rochester at 2 shillings a ton by sea or £6 by land, and the government ordered all shipments by sea must cease. That could have been the death blow to Ipswich's export business, but it was a corpse already.

Few people in Ipswich itself depended directly on cloth-making for a job, and the demise of its chief export affected the town less than the surrounding countryside where most of the clothiers and their workers lived. Although by comparison other exports were insignificant – pewter to Barbados, malt to Norway, skins to Rotterdam – economic activity and living standards were rising in Ipswich as everywhere else. Names from the service industries – carriers, shopkeepers, lawyers, doctors, apothecaries – occur with greater frequency. Thomas Artis was a barber-surgeon whose shop contained 10 razors, 4 wig-blocks, 12 bleeding bowls and a tooth stool. William Blois was a merchant who built a sugar refinery near The Christopher, his home in St Nicholas's parish, importing not direct from Barbados but via London where most of his overseas business was based. Robert Lane, landlord of the Wagon Inn adjoining the Ancient House, started the town's first weekly passenger coach service to London before 1582. (The venture nearly ruined him until he was granted a monopoly, the economic panacea of those days.) The business was still in the family in 1651 when, after the Battle of Worcester, Charles II hid on his way to France in the Ancient House, directed thither by a Lane kinswoman; or so tradition alleges.

Pewter mugs and plates were being replaced by china, and oak furniture by walnut. The windows or more houses and shops were being glazed. More walls were covered with tapestry and more tables with carpet. Clocks, books, mirrors and curtains appeared in more inventories. Under the provisions of Le Domesday, Ipswich families were unaccustomed to primogeniture, and the large fortunes of the previous century had been split up, invested in land or spent. No others were being made on the same scale.

Between 1603 and 1664 the population of town and suburbs doubled to 9,100. Space consequently was at a premium and several schemes were undertaken to ring the dunghills more tightly with housing development. In the town centre, round the Colehill and Hugh Sheale's adjacent salt pit, infilling was allowed on waste land once used for dyeing. Beside the Coldunghill near St Clement's, Sheale, a manufacturer of gunpowder, obtained permission to build himself a big house in exchange for 200lbs of his product, while nearby some more fastidious speculator put up tenements for the poor to rent.

Shipping and shipbuilding were now the growth industries. During the seventeenth century tonnage owned at Ipswich grew six-fold, and the port became the third largest in the country. In addition to many smaller vessels, there were 50 of between 200 and 300 tons, supplying Newcastle coal to London and Suffolk, and later (after Newcastle won

Stoke Mill and Bridge.

back the trade) transporting Suffolk food and cider to satisfy the voracious appetite of the capital.

The main shipyards were near the Common Quay and round the river's bend at what is now Orwell Quay in St Clement's. For the former the town charged a rent of 2 pence per ton built, vastly more commercial than the annual 4 pence once paid by the Bigots. Many of the ships were of 100 tons or more and readily adaptable to war service so as to attract the Crown's building subsidy of 5 shillings a ton. By 1620, 12 ships a year were being constructed, at least one of which was of 600 tons for the East India Company.

The estuary, however, continued to silt up, the highly-rated oak of Suffolk became scarcer, and after the mid-century, construction of the larger ships declined rapidly. London production, with which that of Ipswich had once been comparable, pulled ahead, especially after Henry Johnson of Aldeburgh opened his huge new yard on the Thames instead of the Orwell.

Hemp from Riga and canvas from France were considered the best in Europe, but for a time during its shipbuilding boom, Ipswich 'Mildernex' sailcloth, made from Suffolk hemp – cheaper than the

French and more reliable in supply – was in great demand. Even after Pepys decided the Royal Navy must use Riga hemp, Ipswich sailmakers could surely have carried on by importing that, but they failed to adapt.

Cloth exports were gone, sailmaking was gone, the best of the shipbuilding was gone; the coal trade was gone, but that at least had been replaced. The Town Council made various forlorn attempts to attract other industries, linen and silk-weaving in particular. It was hoped that, offered appropriate inducements, French Huguenots would settle in the town, but only unsuitable types were attracted. A few hat shops were started up, nothing of permanent value. Rich men – no longer concerned to establish chantries for their souls' sake – were encouraged to leave money to a town fund for the provision of 10-year interest-free loans to small businesses. In 1665 £1,000 was available but here too the relevant committee exhibited little talent for spotting winners. Security was required, and possibly its members were too fussy. Ten years later there was £529 in the kitty which, during one of its cash-flow crises, the Corporation borrowed itself, and probably never repaid.

The cloth industry of course was not entirely dead. Local demand in 1661 was providing a living for as many as 19 clothiers in the town. But, especially after the Great Plague of 1666, there was less money around and less ability or determination to do anything about it. Celia Fiennes, a Cromwellian colonel's daughter, a lady with a sharp eye, noted the 'pride and sloth' of Ipswich. Memories of the ample days and profits of the golden fleece were dying hard.

CHAPTER NINE

The Corporation

Cash flow had long been a weakness of the Corporation's accounts. The system, controlled by a Treasurer and the two Chamberlains, (who having been appointed for one year, were concerned to show a surplus for that year) did not distinguish between a debt due and a debt paid. They collected what they could of their predecessors' outstanding debts and it was up to their successors to collect the overspill of theirs. After a number of years, when the arrears total got out of hand, it was written off. No one person could be blamed for that.

This seems to have worked well enough in the middle ages, but in the more complex modern world, after the town became a borough corporate in 1463 (making it a legal person) insolvency was a recurring problem. In 1518, during the unprecedented prosperity of the export boom, the Corporation had difficulty finding the modest £60 tax or geld which had been fixed 200 years earlier at the time of the rewriting of Le Domesday.

During the sixteenth century, the buoyancy of the customs' revenue and the still modest demands of the expenditure account, helped keep the town financially afloat, although there was little surplus cash for emergencies. In the crisis of the Spanish Armada, Portman's Meadow was temporarily mortgaged to charter the two ships required by the Queen for national defence, and mortgaged again to provide a suitable present for Charles II at the Restoration, a no less critical emergency for the Roundhead town.

Direct taxation – such in those days was the beneficent strength of local democracy – was not yet an option for the authorities. Bishop Parkhurst, with difficulty and the bailiffs' help, managed to institute a parish rate in 1572 in order to provide meagre stipends of £8 a year for their clergy, but when his successor wanted to raise them to £40, he needed the support of the Privy Council to force through a higher levy on the parishes. (During the witch-hunting craze in 1645, the jailer complained of the cost of feeding the multitude of penniless old women on remand. A special rate was ordered on the prosecuting parishes, and the jail was soon empty.)

Likewise the Poor Rate, also a parish responsibility, was imposed by Parliament. Four times between 1609 and 1615 the basic figures had to be doubled. The Corporation assisted by selling rye, coal, butter and cheese to the poor at subsidised prices, and at the time of a smallpox outbreak an exceptional rate was raised in St Mary le Tower, St Lawrence's and St Stephen's to help the poorer parishes.

During the Great Plague of 1666, those who could afford to do so, got out of town. In the 10 years following, the population declined from 9,100 to 7,400. The worst affected parishes, where 82 per cent of the fall took place, were those near the river plus the large poor parish of St Margaret's. Colehill Lane in St Nicholas's may have been badly hit, hence perhaps its name-change around this time to Silent Street. It was a busy time for writing off arrears of debt.

The Corporation's income during the seventeenth century seldom reached the level of £1,000 a year. It came from rents, licence fees, local customs' dues and Court fines. In addition, a surprisingly large

The Old Customs House.

sum (sometimes £90) might be raised from the sale of freedoms and from payments for exemption from holding public office. Rents from the town's principal assets, Handford Mill and Farm where the big May and August cattle fairs were held, rose during the century from £60 to £116 a year, rather more than the rate of inflation. Stoke Mill's rent was around £60 for most of the century, and that of the butchers' Shambles on Cornhill grew from £40 to over £60. Portman's Meadow and other odds and ends produced a further £100. Licence fees from publicans, stall-holders in the street markets, and 'foreign' (ie non-freeman) shopkeepers added about £60.

Collection of customs' dues was carried out by the Water Bailiff who paid the Corporation between £30 and £50 for the job each year and kept half the dues; probably all that raised at least another £100, if the man was trustworthy. Samuel Caley was Water Bailiff for the 9 years to 1703 when he was rashly prosecuted for non-payment and eventually awarded substantial damages. It was discovered he had been absenting himself for days on end, leaving open the doors of the customs' warehouse. Then, no doubt to make up the figures, he allegedly drove business away by charging too much – 14 pence for a hogshead of tobacco and 5 pence for a barrel of soap or raisins.

After lead pipes were laid in the 1660's to extend the water supply to 140 households in the centre of town, fees from that brought in £70 a year. Court fines, the Conqueror's 'profits' of jurisdiction, were clearly the largest item of receipts totalling several hundred pounds a year. Were the fines stiffer, one wonders, after a year of heavy expenditure?

Samuel Ward's salary of £120 was the heaviest regular charge on the Corporation. The town clerk, its key official, received only £13 plus 4 shillings for paper and ink. The organist of St Mary le Tower, like the Bailiffs, got £10, and the man who cleaned out the Shambles £2 a year. Repairs to roads, bridges, public buildings, the water conduits, the crane at the quay, and the goose house are other recorded expenses. Restoration of the ramparts in 1642 at the beginning of the Civil War, cost £357, and parties for the Duke of York, the King's brother, £45 after it. From 1560, the militia was another expense.

The waits are a small example of how costs and amenities had escalated. Their job was to keep watch on winter's nights by making music round the town. Fifteenth century documents occasionally record 3 of them costing 13 shillings a year. By the beginning of the seventeenth century there were 6 (5 minstrels and a singing boy) under contract at around £20 a year who were also expected to perform at official functions.

All this, however, was small change compared to the burden of the Civil War. Several thousand pounds annually was raised by Parliament from the people of Ipswich either in direct taxation, loans, or 'voluntary' contributions. You can only squeeze a lemon for so long until the pips squeak. Samuel Dunckon, a militant Puritan, a non-kneelant – ie he refused to kneel at Communion – who had taken on the task of tax collecting when no one else dared to do it, and with his own money had raised and equipped a troop of 74 horse, claimed that he had lent Parliament £300 and supplied the army with £264 worth of biscuits, and that neither debt was ever paid. There were Royalist riots in 1642, and by 1647 public opinion was said to have swung in favour of the King.

Samuel Ward died in 1640 and there was no one else to fire the people's enthusiasm for the Parliamentary cause as he could. Congregations at St Mary le Tower ominously declined. Volunteers for the army and navy were slow to come forward. Fear of the press gangs, as well as Puritan restrictions, emptied the taverns, and a number who were caught were rescued by their neighbours. Piracy on the Orwell and beyond got out of hand, hitting the already shrunken pockets of the merchants and fishermen.

At one stage the town was owed £1,000 or more by the Admiralty for the expenses of looking after 900 sick and wounded sailors, victims of the Dutch war. Able-bodied troops, 'lusty, proper men', for all the damage they did, were less of a financial worry, and in 1657 the bailiffs used the presence of 3 companies of foot and a troop of horse already in billets as an excuse for having no more wounded.

Since the days of Edward I, Ipswich had sent two members to Parliament. It was then an unimportant job for which prominent men, disinterested in local politics, allowed themselves to be elected out of a sense of duty or for the prestige of the thing, like promotion to the House of Lords today. As the status of MPs grew with the Crown's need for money, their electors expected more from them. For 8 years from 1604 Francis Bacon represented the town, the most distinguished man ever to do so, but even he might have been nonplussed by the list of things to put right which was presented to a pair of his successors, Cage and Gurdon, in 1640. It included the unruliness of the Commons, the Irish, poor defence procurement, and corruption – impossible demands, as we know.

The structure of the Town Council or Assembly at the beginning of the seventeenth century had changed little since King John's Charter. The Bailiffs were still elected by the Great Court of all freemen, but since at least 1448 they had been assisted in their judicial capacity in the Portmansmote by 4 JPs chosen from among the 12 portmen, and since 1574 by a Recorder, the chief law officer, a professional lawyer. The Court of the coroners – only 2 since 1317 – was now primarily concerned with inquests post mortem. The portmen and the Council of 24 had for some time elected themselves for life, the portmen's vacancies usually being filled from the 24. The 12 senior members of the latter were called Headboroughs whose main responsibility was to walk round the town once a quarter with their Dirt Books. All these men ran the town through various committees, meeting themselves as a rule once a month. Originally an oligarchy of rich merchants, the Town Council was gradually taken over during the 1600's by shopkeepers and tradesmen.

The Great Court met about half a dozen times a year, starting at 10am and ending at noon. In addition to the town officials, who fixed the agenda, an important instrument of control, normally about 50 freemen attended, out of a total approaching 300. They were expected to be decently dressed, speak through the Chair (a recent innovation) and to use temperate language. When Christopher Ward called the supporters of his opponent knaves and asses, he was find £10 on the spot. Parliamentary elections, on a show of hands, for which 200 might turn up, were held at a Great Court.

For a time during the Civil War, the Great Court had successfully reasserted its ancient right to choose the Council direct,, but this didn't suit Charles II and in 1665 a new Charter restored the pre-war status quo. In addition, all freemen were required to take the Oath of Supremacy. Initially only 37 did so (7 using their mark rather than a signature). Although 15 members of the Council were dismissed and disfranchised as a result of this, within a few years most had either conformed or died.

In 1684, the Great Court was invited to accept yet another Charter which reduced the 24 to 18, replaced 5 portmen with (in effect) Crown nominees, and gave to the Council power to elect the Bailiffs. Naturally this was at first refused, but Judge Christopher Milton (the poet's brother) threatened litigation, and Ipswich gave in. The main points of his rather fatuous arguments were that the Corporation was run by a bunch of fanatics, that the Bailiffs were illegally coining farthings (1/4 pennies), that the Quakers were being allowed out of jail on weekdays and that the town's Courts were not only failing to punish absentees from church (there at least he was wrong: 98 were prosecuted in that year) but were generally unjust. Four years later the 1665 Charter was reinstated, and Ipswich voters were free again to run their own lives. But other gremlins were waiting in the shadows. They were called Whigs and Torys.

CHAPTER TEN

Blue and Yellow

IPSWICH limped into the eighteenth century, its government corrupt and penniless, its population after the Great Plague, static or in decline and facing the new horrors of smallpox and influenza.

In the power vacuum produced by the Glorious Revolution of 1688, corruption had become a national malaise. 'Everyone has his price', said the Prime Minister confidently. It was as bad as anywhere in Ipswich and was to remain so for over a century: 'an ill-regulated republic', the town was called at the time of the Municipal Reform Act of 1835, 'an oligarchy of the worst description'.

A newspaper at the beginning of this period had a piece about an Ipswich family whose physical misfortunes symbolised the moral plight of the whole community. The mother had one arm, and the father one leg. Solomon had been born with one eye, and Roger lost one in an accident. James had one ear, the other having been bitten off by another boy. Matthew had three fingers on one hand, Jonas was lame, and David a hunchback. Only Ezekiel was whole: he saw active service in the army, and having recovered from several wounds, still in his twenties was drowned.

Litigation and corruption go hand in hand and the Corporation was now seldom out of the Courts, for which substantial finance was required. Six hundred pounds was borrowed in 1706 to fund existing debts and to pay the costs and damages awarded to Caley, the Water Bailiff. A further £1,000 was needed in 1707 and £1,200 in 1712. Everything possible was mortgaged, including the Customs House, the Grammar School, the Water Supply and the Town Hall itself, and remained so for some time. Soon the Corporation's regular income was barely sufficient to service the interest payments. But a corporation never goes bankrupt: its electors are always there as a last resort to foot the bill, and at length in 1708 and 1709 £1,600 was raised in a special tax, a portentous step. All of this fell on the freemen alone, the electors who would perforce have voted for it. By the beginning of nineteenth century through the development of the rating system, every resident above a certain wealth-threshold was paying substantial sums, the freemen themselves contributing barely 10 per cent.

From about 1690, freedoms were being sold with indiscriminate abandon. They cost £5 per head, although money was only a secondary consideration. It was their votes which members of the Council were after. In 1650 there had been under 300 freemen: at the Parliamentary election of 1741 over 1,000 voted.

No longer constrained since 1661 to appear annually in person to swear the Whitsun oath, many of these new burgesses lived miles away, especially in London and Kent, but that didn't matter. Some malcontents, having lost an election, petitioned Parliament on the subject, and the Council after more legal costs, won its case. Nevertheless the flow of new freemen was stemmed after 1750.

Every public office, from Town Clerk to Town Crier, was subject to hectic electioneering. Non-resident freemen not only had to be brought to town and returned home afterwards, but entertained while they were here, and of course bribed; (or, far worse, threatened with loss of trade or job, the press gang or physical assault.) One Town Clerk said his election had cost him £350, and another £1,400. The system bankrupted at least two. The secret, obviously, was to make yourself so useful and popular in office that, once there, no one in the following year would think it worth while standing against you, and in this respect the town benefited. William Batley was able to remain Town Clerk, with two intermissions, over a period of 25 years.

Although the candidates rather than the Corporation paid these expenses, they had to be recouped somehow. The Town Clerk's salary was still a nominal one, but his total emoluments by the end of the century were around £500 a year. The Chamberlains at some stage were able to deal a serious blow to the town's revenue by persuading the authorities they should be allowed to keep the Court fines for themselves. And the Corporation accounts, in the care of the Treasurer, sometimes in suspicious circumstances escaped audit.

The portmen and the Council of 24, holding office for life, had an easier time. The Bailiffs themselves, after the upset in 1690 when the Great Court voted overwhelmingly for two non-portmen, began to be chosen from a wider spectrum, with concomitant increases in election costs. Freedoms were a fabulous investment: the Bailiffs were known to pay up to £18 for a vote, and in the next century Parliamentary Candidates sometimes went to £50.

To a growing extent throughout the century these electoral contests were run on party lines, Whigs against Tories, Yellow against Blue. In time everything divided into these colours: taverns, shops, banks, schools even, and church pews. The town's only newspaper in the eighteenth century, the Ipswich Journal, was blue.

The Whiggamores originated as a Scottish Presbyterian sect, and until 1741 Ipswich with its Puritan background was a Whig stronghold. In that year the cantankerous squire of Orwell Park, Old Grog', succeeded in winning one of its Parliamentary seats for the Tories. This was Admiral Vernon[1], a national hero after his victory at Porto Bello, but best remembered now for ordering the Navy to dilute its rum ration with water.

The Admiral held the seat until his death in 1757. Thereafter, for the 17 years to 1784, Staunton and Wollaston returned the sheep of Ipswich to the yellow fold. Colonel Wollaston, who was said to have spent a total of £30,000 on the four elections of that period, was a smart operator, perhaps too smart for his own good. He was one of the first people to spot the talent of Gainsborough, and commissioned his

Colonel Woolaston.

1. Nicknamed from the showerproof cloak and breeches of grogham, made from silk, mohair and wool, which he always wore.

Daundy's Cross and the Town Hall
(The Three Tuns, later the Corn Exchange Tavern on the left)

Greyfriars, 1600 (from the Smart Memorial)

Gainsborough's gardener

St. Clement's, 1600 (from the Smart Memorial)

Ipswich Regatta, about 1895

Prince Albert lays the foundation stone of Ipswich School, 1851

Samuel Ward

portrait from him, a serious mistake if he was expecting to impress posterity with his charm.

Gainsborough, before setting out to achieve fame and fortune in Bath, spent six years at Ipswich with his young family in a rented house in Foundation Street, advertising his profession with a wooden cut-out of a gardener[1] leaning over the fence. His greatest friend in the town, and finally his executor, was Samuel Kilderbee, the town clerk. Gainsborough did a portrait of him too, a witty intelligent face, very different from his depiction of the ambitious colonel.

In 1784, the Whigs and Tories agreed to fix the election by putting forward just one candidate each. Middleton (blue) and Cator (yellow) were duly elected. Alexander Crickitt stood as a maverick Tory and got 7 votes. But he was a banker, and spent his money shrewdly – not to buy votes but to collect evidence that Cator had bought them. Bribery even then was illegal but when disguised as entertainment or help to the needy, hard to prove. Nevertheless Crickitt successfully petitioned Parliament and was granted the seat in Cator's place.

After this memorable achievement, the Napoleonic Wars and the popularity of Pitt kept the Tories almost continuously in power at Ipswich until the notorious election of 1820. By then the town's population and outward appearance were very different.

Nelson had pinpointed the beaches north of Shingle Street as the most likely for an invasion, and troops were moved into Suffolk from all over the country. They were chiefly militia as much of the regular army was abroad. Every parish in Ipswich had already with patriotic fervour fulfilled its militia quota and in 1794, the second year of the war, the town raised an additional Volunteer Corps, the Ipswich Regiment.

Cavalry barracks were put up north of St Matthew's (which became the garrison church) a second to house 7,000 foot soldiers near the top of the Woodbridge Road, and a third in Stoke by the bridge. Thus the population, which had increased in the 50 years before 1801 by about 40 percent to 11,000, was practically doubled overnight. While all the building was going on, troops were billeted in every available tavern whose landlords whinged to the Secretary of State about their loss of earnings. They were told there was a war on; and in any case the extra custom surely benefited them.

Even by modern standard, Cornhill in 1800 must at times have been

1. He is often referred to as Tom Peartree, but this may be an elision with another story: when Gainsborough was living in Sudbury, he saw a man stealing from his orchard. The thief, whom the artist called Tom Peartree, was identified by Gainsborough's drawing of his face.

Samuel Kilderbee.

impossibly congested. Its open space, with a busy corn market round Daundy's Cross at its centre, was still also the town's livestock market. Horses for sale, plus cattle, pigs and sheep mixed with the local traffic and the almost hourly passage of a stage coach. The Shambles at its south-east corner had been supplanted by an overpowering building called the Rotunda – a circle of 30 outwardly-facing shops with a large airless room above, which after its inaugural Ball in 1794 was used as a doss-house for soldiers' families. It was replaced in 1812 by a Regency Corn Exchange that killed two birds with one stone by enabling Daundy's Cross to be removed likewise. The latter's crowning figure of Justice was re-erected as Ceres above the pediment of the Corn Exchange, her sword cleverly beaten into a sickle and her scales into a sheaf of corn.

The Rotunda's shops, along with the stalls which had been cluttering up the streets nearby, were re-located in a new Provisions Market in the southern half of today's Buttermarket shopping precinct. Owned by a private consortium, it comprised an arcaded rectangle like a cloister with the greengrocers grouped in a small central quadrangle round a fountain. To the south, at the top of Silent Street, the consortium bought land for a new Cattle Market, replacing the unsatisfactory site at Tower Ramparts whither the livestock had been cleared from Cornhill six years previously.

A little later, Tavern Street was widened from its original 12 feet by knocking down the buildings on its north side, although The Great White Horse survived with a fine new front. Prigg's Coffee House at the corner of Tower Street with its elaborate carving was demolished, but the Assembly Room adjoining it was left intact. It had been feared that that might have to go as well, and New Rooms were built in Northgate Street to replace it. They were never so popular, and were soon converted into a School of Art. The extraordinary medieval Town Hall was given a smart Palladian facade.

The 1820 Parliamentary election was the closest on record. Over 90 per cent of the electorate voted out of a total still little more than 1,000, of whom two-thirds were non-resident. Haldimand and Lennard were the Whigs' candidates, and Robert Crickitt (Alexander's son) and Round the Tories. As there were two seats, everyone had two votes.

The poll lasted for six days. By the end of Day Two, 325 people had

The Rotunda.

voted, with the Whigs leading by about 30 votes. That evening coachloads of non-resident freemen began to arrive and the price of votes which had been £2 or less for residents, rose to £20 for the newcomers. They were accommodated or 'cooped' in sympathetic taverns and given unlimited supplies of alcohol. Bribery purchased only the promise of a vote, and cooping was necessary to ensure the promise was kept. Like selecting pears, it required precise timing. On Day Three, these cooped electors were brought out, just – but only just – before they became too fuddled to recognise the candidates' names at the polling station.

On Day Four, 59 pairs of votes were cast, and the Tories reduced the gap considerably. Both sides were now struggling so that a number of people were turned away by the returning officers as being under age or not freemen. The Tories, scenting victory, spent Day Five (Saturday) raising enthusiasm round the town with bands and banners, while the Whigs, who polled only 2 votes on that day against the Tories' 11, drowned their gloom in the taverns. On Monday (the last day) the Whigs got 14 votes and the Tories 13. Someone had been dispatched on the Saturday to collect a Whig voter from Bristol, but he arrived too late.

The result, after all, was a double yellow victory. Haldimand received 483 votes, Lennard 482, Crickitt 474 and Round 468. The Tories of course demanded a scrutiny. Their opponents raised no objection, claiming there were about 70 dud Tory votes against the 20 they knew of their own.

In due course the Bailiffs announced the Whigs had lost 55 votes and the Tories 44; and that, in the time-honoured phrase, Crickett with 430 and Haldimand with 428 were duly elected to serve as Members of Parliament for the constituency. Lennard, now with 427 votes, complained with some justice that as the Bailiffs were Tory, their scrutiny was biased, and asked for a professional assessor, but this was refused.

The Whigs' staff-work during the scrutiny had been particularly thorough. One piece of information enabled them to report three cases of Tory electors at Sudbourne near Orford who were suspected of receiving poor relief, and were thus ineligible to vote. The Bailiffs ordered the parish overseer of the poor to produce his books. On the day fixed, a Whig supporter disguised with a blue watch-ribbon and calling himself Mr Goose, rode over to Sudbourne, allegedly to ensure the accounts supported the Tory case. He arrived in time to help the overseer complete writing them all up in a fresh book which omitted any reference to the three Ipswich voters.

Somehow Mr Goose persuaded him to bring both books to Ipswich, keeping the genuine one in his pocket and under oath handing the false one to the Bailiffs. Once the overseer had thoroughly perjured himself, Mr Goose whipped the true book out of his pocket; and, like his accounts, his goose was cooked.

Possibly it was Crickitt's desire to hush up this ugly little scene which persuaded him, after the threat of a Parliamentary investigation and a month of agonising, to give up his seat to Lennard.

It was the custom to 'chair' victorious candidates in a procession. Haldimand, the Whig, had postponed his chairing; but Crickitt, prematurely, had had his and presided over a gala dinner at the Assembly Room, joining in a specially-composed victory chorus 'True Blue Ladies'. Now, for real, it was the Whigs' turn. July 3rd saw Ipswich sparkling everywhere in the sunshine colours of gold and yellow. Even Ceres, in her new perch above the Corn Exchange, was blindfolded with a yellow scarf, sickle and sheaf temporarily transformed again into the sword and scales of Justice.

Cornhill, 1830.

The morning procession, a mile long and divided by three bands, took two hours to traverse the town from St Matthew's to St Clement's and back. It was led by a 'knight' on a grey horse and in armour of polished brass. The heat inside the armour is said to have killed him soon after.

Watched by 400 Whig ladies from a stand in the middle of Cornhill, the chairing of the two Members, now in full evening dress, commenced at 2pm. Each chair was on its own platform, draped in orange, scarlet and purple. They were carried by 20 men round roughly the same circuit in a similar procession to the morning's, and the day ended with the usual victory dinner.

The Whigs reckoned the election had cost them around £40,000, or £2m at today's prices. The bill from The Golden Lion alone, their headquarters beside the Town Hall while The Suffolk Hotel was being rebuilt, was £800. The Tories' total must have been similar. Soon afterwards, Robert Crickitt who had an overdraft even before the election, was declared bankrupt with debts of £58,000.

By now, the town's resident electorate was predominantly composed of poor artisans and labourers, earning perhaps 15 shillings a week, whose vote was by far their most valuable asset. Thus in 1825 a move by the portmen, who had long been all yellow, and the 24, all blue, towards forming a coalition to avoid the expense of elections, was not welcome. A group of Tory freemen, on the pretext that this threatened their 'influence', formed themselves into the Wellington Club, basically to stir up trouble. Its success was immediate: nothing more was heard about coalitions, and for some years, through the Bailiffs and the 24, the Club effectively ran the town.

The Reform Act of 1832 limited the Parliamentary vote to residents who had property worth £10 or more. This cut out all but a handful of Ipswich freemen. However, it in no way altered bribery habits and, as transitional 'relief', existing resident freemen were allowed to retain their vote for life. The electorate of Ipswich rose marginally to 1,219, the new qualifying residents slightly outnumbering the disfranchised non-residents.

Local government was reorganised three years later by the Municipal Reform Act when portmen and 24 were merged into a single Council, and the two Bailiffs replaced by a Mayor, all to be chosen by the ratepayers. (With unusual economy, the Bailiffs' robes were cannibalised into one new set for the Mayor.) A crisis was imminent anyway: the portmen had become powerless since, unwilling to replenish their numbers from their Tory opponents in the 24, their membership had dwindled to 4, below the legal quorum. It is easy to say 'good riddance', but from before Magna Carta to Queen Victoria's accession, the system had worked with minimal change reasonably well. History records only the bad moments.

Bribery remained a potent force in most places until the second Reform Act of 1857 which, with its big increase in the franchise, made the old arrangements impossibly expensive. At Ipswich, the turning point came after the 1835 election for Parliament, and in an unexpected way.

In that year, both seats were won by Tories. The Whigs, as had become almost routine, petitioned for a Parliamentary investigation. Their key witness was a tailor, George Cunnold, who had gone to the poll brandishing four fivers with which he said the Tories had attempted to bribe him. The Tories of course counter-claimed he had been bribed by his own side to say so.

The three-month inquiry uncovered evidence of further corruption. Again, that was routine. This time the difference was that the two candidates were themselves palpably implicated, a hazard which no doubt Crickitt had anticipated when he stood down in 1820. They

The Cartoon that won Fitzroy Kelly the 1837 Election.

were at once unseated and, with their seven accomplices, locked up in Newgate during the Speaker's pleasure. A fresh election, called for the following week, produced a Whig victory.

The culprits' imprisonment lasted 4 months. On his release, Fitzroy 'Applepip' Kelly, one of the two ex-MPs, challenged his Whig opponent, Rigby Wason, to a duel. Wason sneaked to the Speaker and it had to be cancelled. The voters loved it, and a cartoon depicting bantam Kelly (he was a small man) in pursuit of cockerel Wason trailing a white feather from his tail, was thought to have been the deciding factor in winning Kelly back the seat by four votes in 1837. Even so, the scandal caught a mood. Radicalism was in fashion, Nonconformism was riding high, and political corruption was never again a serious issue in Ipswich.

CHAPTER ELEVEN

Taverns and Theatres

IN 1598, at the Privy Council offices, the Court of the Earl Marshall of England sat to hear a case of brawling in Ipswich. But for the Earl Marshall, that too might have led to a duel.

The affair concerned the 25 year old Edmund Withypoll, grandson of the man who had built Christchurch Mansion, and his friend Anthony Felton. It was Felton's habit, gentleman that he was, to allow Withypoll on formal occasions to take precedence because, with £1,000 a year, he was the richer. But one day, going into some reception when husbands were not present, Mrs Withypoll was

Christchurch Mansion, about 1670.

grabbed by Mrs Felton's grandmother and told to let her granddaughter go in first.

Soon afterwards, Withypoll accosted Felton in the town and complained of this insult to his wife. Felton shrugged his shoulders, and Withypoll struck him with his stick. Bystanders joined in the scuffle, Felton drew his sword, and Withypoll escaped to Christchurch and safety.

It took two sessions to hear all the evidence, after which the Earl Marshall pronounced the verdict: Felton was not only a JP but also a captain of horse in the militia, while Withypoll was only a captain of foot. On both counts Felton took precedence, and Withypoll must apologise. If the men ever made it up, did their wives do likewise?

Seventy years later, Charles II came to dinner at Christchurch as the guest of Withypoll's granddaughter, Lady Hereford and her husband. They had just modernised the house after a fire, substituting gables in the Dutch style at the front in place of the simple Tudor ones, adding a porch, and totally remodelling the interior.

It was only months after the Great Plague had emptied many of the town's poorer houses, while not a few of the grander ones, after the collapse of the cloth trade and the departure of the great merchants, were decayed or empty also. The silting-up of the Orwell and the decline of shipbuilding would have added to the general air of dereliction in a town much of whose centre, still covered by large private gardens, seldom seemed crowded at the best of times. It must have been on this occasion that some courtier gave birth to the strained aphorism, barely worthy of its frequent quotation, that Ipswich had a river without water, streets without names and a town without people. Only the asses wore boots, he added, meaning the animals working on the Christchurch bowling green.

A number of the merchants' houses were being turned into taverns about this time. Thomas Eldred's old home in Fore Street became The Neptune, its original name, and what is believed to have been Princess Mary's in Upper Brook Street, The Coach and Horses. The house built by Sir Robert Curson in Silent Street, which later became the Bishop's Palace (and at the time of the King's visit to Christchurch was a military hospital) by the eighteenth century had been further downgraded as The Elephant and Castle.

Another merchant's house in Fore Street, one of the few still intact, was called The Wheatsheaf. Nearby, The Half Moon sported its carved corner post of Friar Fox and the listening geese. Others, in Key

The Coffee House in Tavern Street.

Street, were The Angel, The Bull and The Ram, signs probably associated with their former wealthy owners.

Dog's Head Street was named after The Dog's Head in the Pot, a reference to the Dutch habit of placing the meal of a late arrival on the floor for the dog to eat. Another Dutch tavern was The Galliot Hoy in Fore Street.

In Tavern Street, little trace remained above ground of the great hostelries of Chaucer's relations and their hostmen neighbours. The Mitre at the corner of Dial Lane was on the spot where cousin Albreda had once played hostess at The Holly. Its wine cellar was rediscovered by the Victorians who romantically imagined it might be a subterranean chapel of St Mary Magdalen.

Opposite, at the corner of Tower Street, on the tavern's site where the poet's father had been brought up, was an elaborately decorated building soon to become famous at Harris's Coffee House and Assembly Room (and later, after other name-changes, as Goodings and finally Prigg's) dispensing that 'wakeful and civil drink' just introduced into polite society. There was also Scrutton's in Buttermarket, and Will's behind the Town Hall. Like wine bars today they were considered more up-market than taverns, of which there were now only two or three in Tavern Street. The Chequers, where in Chaucer's poem the Canterbury pilgrims rested, later known as The Rampant Horse and then The Crown and Anchor, was in Westgate Street.

The White Hart in St Lawrence Street, famous for its cooking, was one of the first taverns to have coffee, and much frequented by people waiting for a stage coach. The coach's horn, as it came down Tavern Street, was the signal for coffee to be served at the end of the meal and before the coach passengers dashed in for a cup themselves while the horses were being changed at The Great White Horse.

The history of this establishment (one of the most elegant buildings in Ipswich) goes back to 1518. It was the town's main tavern, and during the eighteenth and nineteenth centuries the centre of Toryism. The Whigs had The Bear and Crown in Westgate Street (opposite The Crown and Anchor) renamed The Suffolk Hotel after a fire. Strictly speaking, both were inns rather than taverns which provided only food and drink, a distinction introduced in the fifteenth century for licencing purposes.

By 1800, 15 stage coaches, including the Royal Mail – at 11.30pm – were entering or leaving Ipswich daily. The Post Office was opposite The Great White Horse. The latter's stabling was reserved for the use of the local gentry, and post-horses were brought down from Neale

Street, by Fonnereau Road, where many of the coaching inns had their stables. Some ran their own, and some, probably the wise ones, used contractors.

George II stayed at The Great White Horse, Louis XVIII had a meal there, and Nelson spent a night there with Lady Hamilton and her husband. Young Charles Dickens was its guest for three weeks while he reported the election of 1835 just before starting to write The Pickwick Papers. Mr Pickwick himself had his adventure among its winding corridors with the lady in the yellow curl papers, and found its public rooms mouldy and its port undrinkable. The landlord threatened to sue Dickens over his comments on the port but thought better of it. Beatrice Webb, staying for a Co-op Congress, and perhaps identifying with Mr Pickwick's lady, thought the hotel romantic.

The eponymous white horse still prances over the entrance porch, 'an insane cart horse', wrote the Whiggish Dickens. He was lucky to have got in at all: inferior applicants for a room, like commercial travellers and even journalists, were often referred down the road to The Royal Oak in Northgate Street.

Cock fighting had been popular for generations, and at least half a

The Great White Horse, 1794.

dozen taverns had specially constructed rooms for the sport, with tiered benches round the central pit, including The Cock and Pye in Upper Brook Street. The Golden Fleece on St Matthew's Corner also had space for bull-baiting. It was the scene of its final appearance in 1805, some years after its commercial practice had ceased on Cornhill. The name Cock and Pye possibly relates to another foible than cock fighting – to the popularity at medieval banquets of Peacock Pie. The bird's tail was fanned out at one end of the pie and its head protruded from the crust at the other. Sometimes its beak was gilded.

The first turnpike was erected on the Claydon Road in 1711, and the increasing road traffic of the eighteenth century brought a second golden age to the taverns of Ipswich. Less than half of those already mentioned can be traced back beyond 1689 when the town had 24 licenced inns plus an unknown number of simple ale-houses. The Greyhound, next to The Cock and Pye, was one of the town's largest when it and The Cross Keys of Carr Street among others, had troops billeted on them in 1650. The Woolpack in Bolton Lane leading north from the Thingstead, the medieval centre of the wool trade, was on one of the oldest sites of all.

Contrary to what Charles II was told, Ipswich streets did have names by then, many of obvious derivation, a few commemorating residents long departed, like Carr, Major or Tacket. On the other hand, legal documents were still liable to omit all reference to streets, so the King's informant may have been thinking of that.

Between about 1700 and 1780 Tacket Street was known as Tankard Street when, possibly as a result of pressure from members of its Congregational chapel, it reverted to its ancient name. In 1736 an entrepreneur called Betts acquired the Wingfields' old house – its great parlour then being used for dancing classes – and converted it into yet another tavern, naming it The Tankard after the street. Beside it, he built the New Theatre.

Secular drama at Ipswich, as distinct from that of the Corpus Christi festival, is first mentioned in 1530 when the Earl of Derby's Players visited the town. Mr Scott's Lads performed something in 1564, and between 1561 and 1588, the Earl of Leicester's Players came 15 times. The Lord Chamberlain's Men, the company of which Shakespeare was a member, came on 4 occasions during his working lifetime, but there is no evidence that they were ever accompanied by the great man himself.

Performances took place in the Town Hall or in private houses or, after 1700, in the new Shire Hall off Foundation Street. For a time, before the New Theatre opened, they were also held at The Griffin tavern adjoining The Rampant Horse in Westgate Street.

The price of seats originally ranged from a penny to a shilling and the company's 'reward' or fee from 13 shillings to £1. The Lord Chamberlain's Men received a quite exceptional £2 in 1595: Shakespeare's latest London hit was The Taming of the Shrew, and it would be nice to think that they got it for that. Fee and box office were divided among the principal actors, out of which the rest of the company were paid salaries of up to 10 shillings a week. Preference was given to husband and wife teams because they came cheaper.

In 1608, under the stern influence of Samuel Ward, the Bailiffs issued an order fining anyone who attended a play or 'loitered' in a tavern. The Prince's Players had to be given £2 in that year as a cancellation fee. Nearly 40 years later, Parliament followed Ipswich's lead and pronounced that all theatrical performances (along with the celebration of Christmas and Easter) were to be illegal, a dam swept away by a sparkling flood of comedy at the Restoration.

The bill of the New Theatre from the beginning offered playgoers rather more than they had been accustomed to, and in the cheaper seats they paid highly for it. Prices now ranged from 30 pence (in real terms comparable to the old top rate) down to a shilling. For this they got not only the main play, followed by a farce or opera, but also singing and dancing in the intervals, sometimes accompanied by the organist of St Mary le Tower on the harpsichord.

One of the biggest early successes was Oroonoko in 1741 in which the show was stolen by a young newcomer, fresh from a job in his uncle's wine shop, David Garrick. After appearing with equal acclaim in several other plays the same month, he returned to London, never to look back; and never once to revisit the scene of his first triumph.

The Norwich Comedians became the regular repertory company and in 1759 took a lease on the theatre. They came for about a month in summer which included Race Week, and for 2 or 3 weeks at Christmas. Plays were sometimes 'bespoken' or sponsored by an individual or organisation such as an officers' mess. Once a girls' school ordered a production of King Lear with a happy ending.

Ipswich had its own way of staging Shakespeare's masterpieces. The gravedigger in Hamlet always brought the house down with well-anticipated stage business, taking off layer after layer of waistcoats before getting down to work. There was often a grand chorus of witches in MacBeth, and at Juliet's funeral an elaborate dirge; while the Comedy of Errors, 'adapted for the stage', included a trip to Brighton. Miss Edmead won great applause in the name part of Hamlet, as did Mrs Ibbot as Falstaff. And at one period of national crisis, an actor appeared as the Shade of Shakespeare himself, leaning on a pedestal as in his memorial in Westminster Abbey, to give his verse analysis of the situation. But one mustn't be too superior: television has surely produced solecisms no less notable.

With humbler dramatists, the town's taste tended towards the melodramatic or sentimental: Castle Spectre (often revived) or Passion's Paradise or The Phantom Bride; or East Lynne with its famous line of 'Dead, dead and never called me mother', or Bound to Succeed with its thrilling climax of an explosion of dynamite.

The zenith of the New Theatre's prosperity came during the Napoleonic Wars when up to 9,000 soldiers were stationed in the town. The box office could afford to be generous, and charity nights were held to buy flannel waistcoats for the troops in Europe or to release favoured debtors from prison. Rule Britannia was played with God Save the King at every performance.

The Tavern Street Assembly Room interior, photographed after it had been taken over by the Working Men's College.

In 1803 the theatre was rebuilt on a more lavish scale and with a larger stage. A few months later it was in mourning for the death of Lord Chedworth, a wealthy bachelor and a great admirer of both the theatre and its actresses. In modern terms he left about £20m. Most of the beneficiaries of his will were ladies, who received up to £1m each in today's currency. They included Mrs Edgar, daughter of the landlord of The Griffin, which still maintained its theatrical links, and Miss Edmead, the acclaimed Hamlet. A Mr Barney, his Lordship's cheesemonger and whist partner, got the equivalent of £200,000.

After the war, the theatre's fortunes declined. Other halls became available, like the Corn Exchange and the Mechanics' Institute and, from 1868, the vast Public Hall in Westgate Street, while the arrival of the railway brought the diversity of London's theatreland so much nearer. It changed hands in 1848, but refurbishment and a fresh name – the Theatre Royal – failed to stop the rot. In 1890 it was purchased by the Salvation Army as a citadel.

The proceeds of the sale went towards the construction of the Lyceum on the site recently vacated by the East Anglian Daily Times in Carr Street. The original stage of the New Theatre had been 30 feet wide by 12 deep: the Lyceum's was 34 by 43, raked in the new style towards the yellow and gold of its auditorium, seating 1,400 and plastered with banal mottoes like All the World's a Stage.

The Lyceum's promise was soon thwarted by the new Theatre of Varieties, the Hippodrome, of St Nicholas Street. Everything was tried to regain the crowds, from the old fare of creepies and weepies to grand opera, concerts and American musicals and movies, but it never made money. It was once put into receivership when it was rashly bought by the Hippodrome's owner. No grants then to see a management through its difficulties. They spoke of bringing culture and enlightenment to Ipswich, dangerous words if the commercial spark was lacking. 'It's up to you', the company's President told the audience with unconscious irony in 1936 on the last night.

Race Week took place every summer from 1727. The gentry came into Ipswich for this social highlight of the town's year culminating, after a series of public breakfasts, plays, concerts, routs and fireworks, with the Race Ball at the Tavern street Assembly Room, or, after 1821, at the new Rooms in Northgate Street.

The Assembly Room in Tavern Street (15 feet by 60) was more like a wide corridor than a room, but satisfactory enough if you were not

The Racecourse.

fussed about space or style. A young Frenchman who visited the town in 1784, noted that local dancers, lacking rhythm, did not distinguish between a quadrille and a minuet, and was surprised to learn that a young man was expected to keep the same partner for the whole evening 'and follow her about everywhere and fetch her tea etc'. He failed to discover a single tavern in Ipswich which was up to the standards back home.

Admittance to the public stand on the 4 mile course between the Felixstowe and Nacton Roads cost 6 pence, and to the Gentlemen's stand 30 pence. The races were few and, because the rules were fewer, run in heats. The King's Plate was worth 100 guineas (£105), the Town Cup £70 and the Town Purse £40. The Ship tavern in Back Hamlet beyond St Clement's, provided stabling for competing horses, as many as 14 in 1772.

Interest fell after Waterloo in 1815. As with the theatre, this was partly due to the growth of the nonconformists, for whom cock fighting was said to be the major attraction, and partly to the shrinkage of the garrison. In 1832 Race Days were reduced from three to two and, to suit the gentry, the first race started at 2pm rather than at 5 o'clock as previously. Once, only two horses turned up to run for the Town Purse and the race was cancelled. Another time, there was just one: he walked round the course and was declared the winner.

The last Meeting was held in 1883. What had originally been a piece of waste heathland used by gypsies was becoming too valuable, and after some years as a steeplechase course, the Council bought it for housing development.

CHAPTER TWELVE

The Nonconformists

PREACHING, like acting, is an ephemeral art, not to be recaptured by the printed word. Perhaps nowhere else was it practiced with wider impact than by the eighteenth and nineteenth-century ministers of nonconformist Ipswich. Formerly, the great Samuel Ward had carried the torch almost alone. Now there were many of them, Congregationalists, Unitarians, Quakers, Baptists, Presbyterians and Methodists whose differing interpretations of the Christian message sparkled with shifting light on a swelling sea of faith, a restless spirituality. It is easy to deride the dissensions created by these good and eloquent men, but they were merely responding to the multifarious demands of increasingly educated congregations who were no longer prepared to take their souls' welfare on trust; and who looked forward to the drama of their Sunday services with a wholesome piety.

Old Mr Notcutt, the third Pastor of the Tacket Street Congregational Church (Christ Church) retired in 1754. His wife died soon afterwards from a nose-bleed. Forty years earlier, she had dreamt that she would, in that very year and in a house exactly like their present one. She had made a full note in her diary. When her nose began to bleed, she remembered the dream and, having verified the details, was able to warn her doctor that he was wasting his time.

Mr Notcutt was followed by William Gordon who eventually emigrated to America and became private secretary to George Washington. David Edwards succeeded Dr Gordon in a ministry of twenty-six years which began and ended in high drama.

One of his first jobs was to visit two young men in prison awaiting execution for housebreaking. Their response to his teaching was such that he got the idea for a sermon, and obtained permission for them to hear him deliver it in Tacket Street (or Tankard Street as it was then) on the eve of their execution. The word got around, and the church which held 800 was packed. They prayed and sang some hymns until the prisoners arrived and were led in chains to their seats. The Pastor's

The Rev. Mr. Notcutt (an engraving from the oil painting damaged by Miss Edwards).

address was frequently interrupted while he broke down in tears. The prisoners did likewise, and soon there was not a dry eye in the house.

Afterwards the young men asked if he would attend them at the gallows on the following morning. 'I told them I could not bear it', and he explained that this was the duty of their parish priest and it would be unprecedented for a dissenting minister to share the occasion.

About 10am the next day a message from the prisoners arrived at the Manse repeating their request. It turned out that it was no longer Church of England practice in Ipswich for a clergyman to be present at a hanging unless invited, so Mr Edwards hired a carriage and set off for Rushmere, soon overtaking the prisoners' cart. He rode with them for nearly a mile but it was so uncomfortable that he returned to his carriage.

There was a large crowd round the gallows tree– like the Last Judgement he reflected – and he asked the deputy Sheriff if he might address them. 'With all my heart', he replied, 'Take your time. Your time shall be mine.' He climbed again into the cart, standing astride with one foot on each of the awaiting coffins. His sermon was on the text 'Flee, youthful lusts' which he preceded with a rendering of The Lamentation of a Sinner, sung to the Windsor tune. Again, not a dry eye. Then he knelt and prayed privately with the two men. Each made a final speech, and the deed was done.

Mr Edwards preached his last sermon in Tacket Street at Christmas 1791 to a divided and depleted congregation.

He had two daughters of marriageable age at that time whom some of the church's membership considered he had allowed to become too familiar with the soldiery. One day these girls were accosted by the Misses Notcutt, granddaughters of the former Pastor, in the vestry at Tacket Street, one of whom pointed to her grandfather's portrait and asked what *he* would have thought of their behaviour. A Miss Edwards answered she was sick of hearing about the old man and thrust her umbrella through the canvas missing his right eye by a few inches.

The sensation caused by this action is not hard to imagine and, after a close vote, Mr Edwards was asked to resign. Many of his supporters left at the same time, and under another minister built a Meeting House at the bottom of Fonnereau Road. They moved again in 1829 to a new Meeting House in St Nicholas Street, and sold the old one to some Baptists, themselves a break-away group from Stoke Green. It became the Bethesda chapel, and was replaced by today's larger building in 1913.

After the long ministry of Charles Atkinson, another sufferer from nose-bleeds which were liable to disrupt his sermons, William Notcutt, nephew of the protagonists of the vestry encounter, became Pastor at Tacket Street. He resigned without warning in 1854, and following an interval, an ex-missionary called William Clarkson was elected. He treated the faithful like his former congregation in the South Seas, upsetting everybody with his brusque manner, refusing to conduct afternoon services, and demanding their dear old church should be rebuilt because its stuffiness was affecting his health. Within a year he was replaced by a fervent Welshman, Eliezer Jones.

Mr Jones made the rebuilding of both church and Manse a condition of his coming. A fashionable architect was hired, Frederick Barnes, a ruthless gothic improver of the town's heritage, and in 1858 the present church was dedicated. This was to have been done by William Notcutt, but he died the day before. Curiously enough, a similar fate had befallen Mr Glandfield, the then Pastor, just before his own planned dedication of the original church in 1720.

Earlier, during the 1680's, after a generation of intermittent persecution, the Congregationalists had been part of a 300-strong community of nonconformists – a Union of Hearts rather than a Vicinity of Houses– until in 1686, after some disagreement, they broke free and rented a Meeting house in St Peter's parish. In 1718, membership having risen from 47 to around 200, they purchased a substantial property in Tacket Street. Its house became the Manse (Mr Glandfield's salary was £84, more than most of the Protestant clergy's in Ipswich) and the church was built behind in his spacious garden.

The other main group of nonconformists were Presbyterians. After the desertion of their Congregationalist brethren, they met in an 'upper room' in Silent Street. In 1700 they bought some land in Friars Street and erected on it their fine Meeting House, a tiny song-thrush now incongruously sited beneath the sleek raven of the Willis Corroon building. Its talented architect is unknown, it is not impossible he was a pupil of Wren, and certainly the elaborate carving of the pulpit (bleakly criticised at the time as unseemly) is likely to have been from the workshop of Grindling Gibbons.

Thomas Scott, its minister between 1737 and 1766, matched the fame of his best-selling verse translation of the Book of Job with the skill with which he and his successors managed their members' gradual

Tacket Street Congregational Church with its original spires, 1860.

transition to unorthodoxy, so that by the turn of the century, with a minimum of fuss, the little Presbyterian thrush of Friars Street, now accompanied by an organ, had become the Unitarian Meeting House.

'One God at most' was the central belief of what someone called 'these rational religionists', among whom men tended to be in the majority. No tears here or long services. Difficult questioners from other persuasions were referred to them – Mrs Martha Ruffel, for example from Tacket Street, who wanted reassurance on the personal coming of the Lord.

Unitarian ministers now came and went with some speed. Mr Jervis lasted for 5 years, Mr Parker for 6, and Mr Rees for 2. Mr Philip died, aged 28, after 2 years and Mr Melville was dismissed in 1833 after 6 years for not paying his debts, while membership sank to an all-time low.

The next minister was Joseph Ketley who within 18 months had increased attendance to 200 on Sunday mornings and to 700 in the evenings, when tea was served. Gin and water, 'one glass and one only', was reserved for vestry meetings.

One day in 1836, amid the tinkling of teacups and the drinking of toasts (another novelty) Mr Ketley dropped his bombshell: he had changed his mind about the depravity of man – i.e. he is depraved. Everyone said he was mad (he had in fact spent some time in an asylum) and he was hastily dismissed, in due course becoming a Protestant priest.

In the same year another nonconformist banner was raised by Thomas Middleditch at the Baptists' former Salem chapel in St George's Street. Its founding Pastor having died, it had been standing empty for 7 years. Mr Middleditch's ministry was not a long one: he was said to lack unction and his membership, an explosive mixture of Baptists and Congregationalists, failed to grow as expected. His successor after threatened litigation by his Baptist flock, commissioned Mr Barnes to design a new chapel in his usual manner down the road at the western end of Crown Street, and moved thither with his Congregationalist members in 1865. The Baptists remaining eventually sold the Salem chapel to be incorporated into the new High Street museum (and later to be converted into the Wolsey Studio) and joined their brethren in Turret Lane.

The Baptists' first Meeting House of Stoke Green, a charming conversion of 6 cottages in a field at Maidenhall, was founded in 1773. Baptisms originally took place in the Orwell at a smuggler's cottage – Cat House at Woolverstone; later in the brook at Freston, and after

The Stoke Green Baptist Chapel, about 1800.

1815 in a bath within the chapel itself. The outdoor crowd had become too noisy, and the candidates' ardour was noticeably cooled when on occasions the river's ice had to be broken.

By 1851, when a count was taken on a wet Sunday in March, nearly 1,900 people were attending Baptist services in Ipswich, rather more than all the other nonconformists put together. Including Stoke Green, there were 4 Baptist churches in the town at this time, the others being the Zoar chapel near St Helen's, Turret Green chapel in Turret Lane, and the Bethesda at Fonnereau Road. As many others, like the old Salem chapel, had come and gone. Another was added in Burlington Street in 1861 by the sacked ex-missionary of Tacket Street, William Clarkson, which was greatly enlarged in 1875 by the arrival of Mr Morris with half his congregation of 400 from Turret Green after a row there.

John Wesley visited Ipswich in 1790 for half an hour, an unscheduled stop on his way to Norwich. The town's first Methodist minister, in 1808, was a timid young man called Thomas Morgan, and its second, a few months later, Richard Pilter, who quickly made his mark by preaching to a large crowd on Cornhill. This service was stopped by the authorities (when they all trooped off to finish it in the meadow, the later arboretum, off the Henley Road) but it had the effect of doubling membership to 50. By 1818 it was 486, and at the 1851 count, after the Wesleyan Association had broken away in 1834 and the Primitive Methodists in 1839, the total number of all varieties of Methodism attending church was 467.

The Methodist church in Museum Street – itself a new road – was opened in 1861. The congregation was a poor one (married ministers were paid £34 a year and unmarried £17) with the lucky exception of one member of the congregation, William Pretty, who donated £1,000 to its building, reportedly his life's savings. (He made it all back in the corsetry business and died a rich man.)

Like Wesley, George Fox the Quakers' founder, visited Ipswich once only. 'I had a little meeting', he wrote in 1655, 'very rude'. Quakers at that period had a reputation everywhere of being uncouth, and it is interesting he found it worth mentioning in Ipswich. They had already been described here, probably at a Portmanstmote as 'dissolute, idle and loose'. After Fox's departure, a number were sent to prison where conditions were so bad that they complained about them to Cromwell who, no doubt to their astonishment, ordered them to be released. In 1660, 23 were in jail and in 1685 43, the men and women whose lax confinement had been noted by Christopher Milton.

In 1700 the Quakers built a small Meeting House near St Mary Quay, and a larger one 100 years later on roughly the same site. Like the other churches, they had their arguments, and in 1836 a splinter group started a chapel in Friars Street, which was soon taken over by the Primitive Methodists. With such a choice of worship, and perhaps old memories of their anti-Puritanism, Ipswich never really took to the Quakers. In 1851 barely 100 of them were regular churchgoers.

Another church census was carried out in October 1881. Evening service was chosen because numbers were usually greater, especially on that Sunday when heavy morning showers had given way to a dry spell. Since 1851, the town's population had risen from 33,000 to 50,000. Church of England attendance, where over half were Evangelical, had increased from 5,700 to 6,600, while that of the nonconformists had doubled. The Methodists had almost trebled their total to more than 1,200 and the Congregationalists, Presbyterians and Unitarians together had raised theirs from about 1,000 to over 2,000. Much of this had been due to the influx of Scots in the 1860's for whom the ubiquitous Mr Barnes designed a Presbyterian church in

Portman Road. The Baptists had seen an increase of 30 per cent in their numbers, and the Quakers a similar fall.

The Methodists by 1881 had built a chapel at Alan Street near Holywell's Park and were soon to open another in Bramford Road and the People's Hall in Stoke. Between 1854 and 1904, the Congregationalists started 4 churches in, and on the way to, California, the new eastern suburb beyond the Felixstowe railway.

By the end of the nineteenth century, the diaspora of the town's great Puritan inheritance was complete. The exciting days of expansion and division, of flowing beards and sermons, thunderous pulpits and copious tears, were over. Their once beloved churches, stern, assertive and hard to heat, remain as grimy reminders of the faith that built them. Their twentieth-century worshippers have found a winding and wider path to salvation, across which the rapiers of theological debate throw a fainter shadow. And after 300 years, among more docile congregations, the mood of unity is once again in the air.

CHAPTER THIRTEEN

Big Business

WHEN David Edwards invited the two housebreakers to visit his church in Tacket Street on the day before their execution, he sought permission from the Sheriff, John Barnard.

In 1719, Barnard, probably encouraged by his widowed stepmother since he was then barely 15, had been the church's main benefactor, donating cash, an expensive chandelier and a pair of old masts to support the roof. He followed his father into the shipbuilding trade and, by the time Mr Edwards was Pastor, was a wealthy man.

During the busy days of the early seventeenth century, there had been seven shipyards at Ipswich, and these, 100 years later, were still ticking over, producing mostly small fishing and coastal vessels: two were close to either end of Stoke Bridge, a couple more a mile or so downstream roughly opposite each other, and three – the most important – in St Clement's where the river's sharp bend brought the deep channel close inshore. It was at one of the latter that Barnard started in business.

Decent orders were hard to come by. Prizes seized in the Dutch Wars had created a surplus of merchantmen, while the Royal Navy, having its own dockyards, only in emergencies employed favoured outsiders. Thus in 1677, when urgent orders were placed for 30 men-o'-war, not one came to Ipswich. At the time, the Orwell was probably considered too vulnerable. In that year 1,000 Dutch troops landed near Felixstowe and attacked the Landguard Fort opposite Harwich. (They retreated when two small ships cleverly fired, not at them, but into the shingle, sowing confusion with the resultant shrapnel of broken stones.)

Barnard, nevertheless, cultivated the Navy Board, and in 1739 was rewarded by a visit from its top brass to see the launching of an unsinkable ship he had just completed. As she hit the water she was holed by a sunken pile, 'whereby the whole design was defeated'.

Undaunted, he successfully pressed for the order to build the

Biddeford, 423 tons and then, at £12 a ton, the *Hampshire*, 854 tons. He quoted £10.50 a ton for a third ship but was over a pound too high.

He took a lease of the Royal Naval dockyard at Harwich in 1742 and, after that, built all his fighting ships there. A few years later, he paid £140 for the old yard downstream on the Stoke site of the river, and named it Nova Scotia in honour of a relation who had just emigrated. Soon after, he added the new Halifax yard a quarter mile beyond.

For over 40 years, with inevitable ups and downs, Barnard prospered. He prudently diversified by putting a tenant into the Nova Scotia yard and in 1767 by converting part of his St Clement's yard into Salt Water Baths. The entrance fee was one shilling, and an annual subscription, 21 shillings.

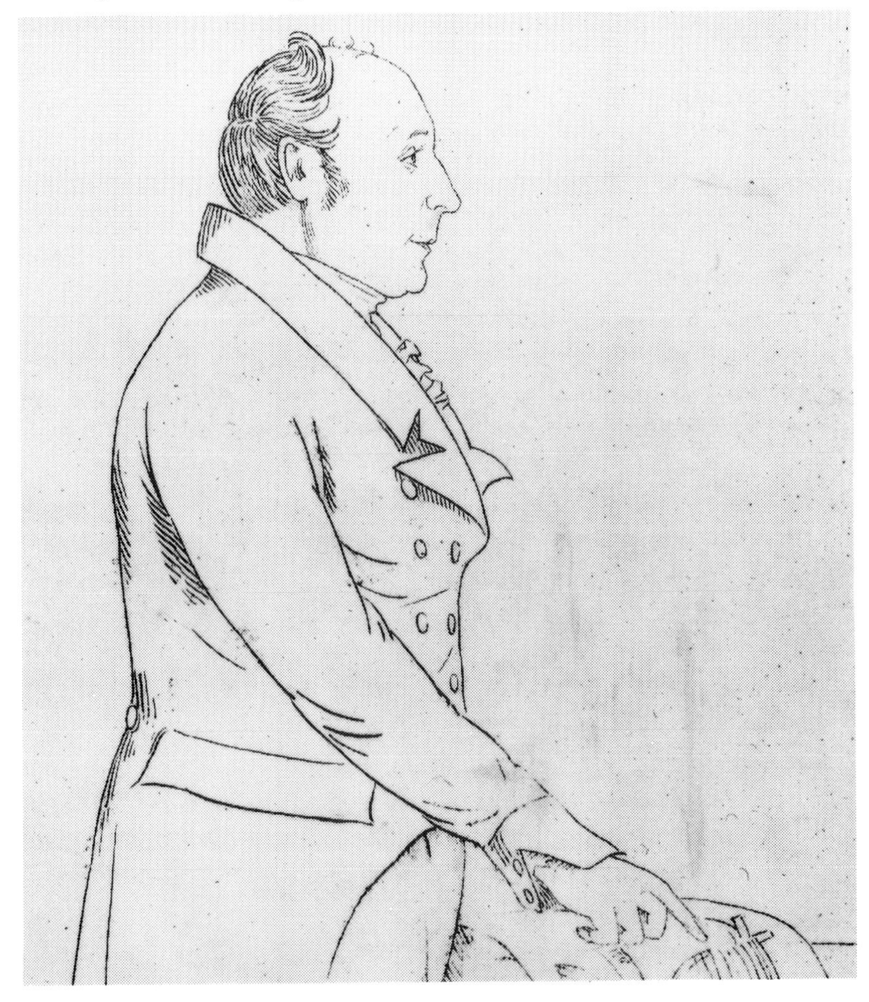

Jabez Bayley.

He was still building ships at the age of 77 when he went bankrupt and spent the last two years of his life at Deptford where his son had set up his own business as a shipwright.

John Bayley, Barnard's tenant of 20 years at Nova Scotia, died a few months later. Mrs Bayley continued the business for another 20, and in 1807 their son, Jabez, took charge.

The war against Napoleon was at its height, prices were rising and demand was strong. Between 1801 and 1814, Bayley's yards produced 31 ships for the Royal Navy and a fortune of £14,000 for Jabez. He was a flamboyant and impulsive man, good-natured but unreliable, according to his nephew George. George added that his uncle was 'susceptible to flattery', and it was in fact his vanity that was to prove his undoing.

George's trenchant comments on his family have made the Bayleys slightly more than mere names. His other uncle, Philip, was also a shipwright but 'not overstocked with brains . . . with a working man's thoughts and habits' and he remained all his life as a labourer in the family business. George wrote of himself, after he had left boarding school at the age of 14 to become Jabez's apprentice: 'but for the shame, I should have given it up – the labour was so much beyond my expectations and physical strength that I about despaired of ever acquiring the practical skills for its successful application'.

His father had died when he was 9, and he spent the first two years of his apprenticeship under Jabez's roof. Then Jabez married, as his third wife, a woman of 'avaricious and grasping disposition', so George moved out. He had inherited the yard near Stoke Bridge (south side) which until his 24th year was managed by Jabez as part of the family firm, with George working as foreman. He took it over in 1821 at his uncle's insistence, and within 6 months had lost half his capital of £1,500. He struggled for 10 years before giving up while still just solvent.

He was married by then and the family home had to be sold. He and his wife stayed with relations while the children were split up and boarded out with neighbours. He fitted out again his shipwright's tool box and, although he never had to use it, he always kept it as a reminder of what might have been. Times were hard, and there was no question of rejoining Uncle Jabez. Refusing many offers of financial help – saying that if he couldn't succeed with his own money, he was unlikely to do so with someone else's – he took a job as Master of the new twice-weekly ferry between Ipswich and London, a wooden steamer recently built at his own yard.

He soon saved £80 which enabled the family to move to Saffron Walden for two terrible years when he worked as a bank clerk. Thereafter he found his feet in London, first as a surveyor for Lloyd's, and finally as a marine consultant on his own account.

Meanwhile, easy success during the ideal conditions of wartime had convinced Jabez that in the harsher climate of peace he possessed the golden touch. He was already operating from the Halifax and Nova Scotia yards in addition to George's at Stoke, and now conceived the idea of acquiring an Ipswich monopoly by taking over the dilapidated yards at St Clement's as well.

His finest hour came in 1817 when, watched by a crowd said to number 20,000, the 1,300 ton East Indiaman, *Orwell*, was launched at the Halifax yard. She was really too big for its limited resources and the yard had to be enlarged and the river dredged to take her, operations which ate up all the profits, and more, on the contract price of £22.50 per ton. Only two further orders in the following year for similar ships got him temporarily out of trouble.

In 1825 he was declared bankrupt, having lost in 11 years the fortune he had made in 12. He later started up again at Stoke, but his

Dykes Alexander.

death in 1835 marked the end of large-scale shipbuilding in Ipswich. The Orwell had little to offer the larger ships of the age of iron and steam.

Forty years earlier, after the death of John Barnard, the Nova Scotia yard had been briefly occupied by the firm of Cornwell and Mangles as a base for their two Greenland whalers. The company's cash was raised by public subscription. The result after three years was a tiny profit and a lot of bickering.

Emerson Cornwell was a partner in the yellow (Whig) bank of Alexander and Cornwell. Both men were Quakers (Dykes Alexander's gardener founded the New Jerusalem church in the High Street) and the bank was situated near the Quakers' Meeting House by St Mary Quay, moving to the top of Princes Street in the 1860's.

The blue bank opened in Tavern Street in the same year as the subscription list for Cornwell's whaling company, 1786. Initially it was called Crickitt, Truelove and Kerridge – the senior partner was the Tory MP, Alexander Crickitt – and then Crickitt, Bacon and Co, and in 1825 after Alexander's death and young Robert's bankruptcy following the 1820 election, Bacon, Cobbold and Rodwell. Rodwell was a local solicitor whose services were no doubt required to sort out Robert's overdraft secured on his father's estate. (Later, Alexander's bank was merged with Barclays and Crickitt's with Lloyds.)

By 1825 there were few pies in Ipswich into which the Cobbolds had not inserted a finger. This was due as much to their fertility as to their commercial enterprise. Old Thomas Cobbold who with his father had transferred the family brewery from Harwich to the 'Cliff' below Holywell's Park in 1746, had only 5 children, but his son John had 21, and his grandson, also John, (one of the two Cobbolds who joined Crickitt's bank) had 14.

The purity of Holywell's water, flowing beside the ruins of the medieval palace of the Bishops of Norwich, was legendary; and the Cobbolds who had owned the property since 1689, had for some years laboriously transported it to Harwich. Thomas's idea of bringing the brewery to the water was so simple that no one previously seems to have considered it.

At the opposite end of town by St George's Street there was another well, a chalybeate spring, holier than Holywell if, as is likely, it had once been associated with the miraculous Madonna of Lady Lane a few yards to the south. The suggestion was made to the owner, Dykes Alexander, that he should develop it as a rival to Cheltenham but he excused himself on the grounds that this would raise prices everywhere by encouraging visitors. The real reason no doubt was the earlier failure of Mrs Martha Coward to make money out of her 'Ipswich Spa Waters' from a similar spring near St Margaret's Green.

Ipswich already had some of the attributes of a spa town. Shipbuilding was the only serious industry to sully its aspect, and that was confined to the edge of town. Lord Oxford wrote in 1737 that the place was 'extremely pleasant and healthy' and very merry with its balls and assemblies. Many business people had retired there, he said, and Defoe added that, although there were fewer gentry than at Bury, the 'solid' residents of Ipswich were more interesting and better informed. Sadly for us, however, this excluded any initiative to replan the town in an elegant contemporary style.

John Cobbold, the elder, took over the brewery on Thomas's death in 1777, and remained its head until his own, in his 90th year, in 1835. Brewing at that period was the route (in Dr Johnson's phrase) to wealth beyond the dreams of avarice, and John exploited his opportunities to the full. He was helped of course by the explosion of the drinking population after the garrison's arrival in 1793. By the time he died, the Cobbolds owned 47 out of the town's 101 licenced premises

Cliff House, beside the Brewery.

half of which doubled up as brothels. Much of the fine panelling and other appurtenances of their prosperous Tudor owners found their way into the house he built for himself at Holywell's Park.

John's second wife, Elizabeth, who presented him with 7 of his 21 children, was a lady of theatrical background and artistic inclination, and a friend of Constable. One summer's evening while they were sketching in the grounds of Cliff House (it was before Holywell's was built) Mrs Cobbold was approached by a young woman looking for a job. Her references were excellent, and she was given employment in the kitchen.

Her boyfriend of some years' standing was a smuggler called Will who for professional reasons was reluctant to settle down and get married, until one day while working for the Cobbolds she got a

Mrs. Elizabeth Cobbold.

message to come to him at once in London, as she guessed for that purpose. A farmer's daughter, she helped herself to one of John Cobbold's best horses and set off. She was caught before she met Will, brought home and sentenced to death. At Mrs Cobbold's intercession this was commuted to seven years' imprisonment. With Will's assistance she escaped, but was caught again. Will was shot in the chase and died in her arms. This time her death sentence was reduced to transportation to Australia where she lived happily ever after.

Stripped of its quivering romantic flesh, such is the skeleton of the tale of Margaret Catchpole. It has all but one of the ingredients any novelist could hope for, and Elizabeth's son, the Rev Richard Cobbold, made the most of them when 50 years later he published his famous 'history', a skilful blend of fact and fiction. The big lie is that Margaret was 35 when she entered the Cobbolds' service, and not 25 or less as in Richard's version.

In 1803 Robert Ransome made the discovery which was to lay the foundation of his family's fortune and permanently to alter the face of Ipswich. He had already patented a cast-iron ploughshare, cheaper and, as he maintained, better than the wrought iron varieties on the

Robert Ransome.

market, before moving with his young family from Norwich to Ipswich in 1789.

It was in the shed, a former maltings, which he rented at the southern end of St Margaret's Ditches – now Old Foundry Road – that one day he noticed that molten iron spilling over from a mould cooled faster, and achieved a greater hardness, if it fell on pieces of cold metal rather than directly on the floor. Within 5 years his new ploughshare with a hardened self-sharpening under-surface dominated the market, and enabled him to standardise his plough parts to be interchangeable in the farmyard, something that local habits and prejudice had previously made impossible. That of course meant longer and more efficient production runs.

Ransome had come to Ipswich with capital of £200: by 1809 when his elder son James moved from Yarmouth to join him, the firm's capital was £3,776. They shared the profits 50/50. It seems unlikely that initially either of them earned more than £200 to £300 a year, say around £10,000 today.

During the next six years, turnover doubled to about £10,000, partly thanks to the arrival in 1812 of a struggling millwright, William

The new Gas works, 1822.

Cubbitt. Robert was now in his 60th year, James's inventive skills were not pronounced, and the talented Cubbitt was a fortunate acquisition. In the nick of time, before the agricultural depression in the aftermath of Waterloo, which might well have ruined the firm like so many others, he took Ransomes into new and unimagined areas: making the self-regulating gear for windmills, constructing treadmills – both his own inventions – and building bridges. By a stroke of luck, Stoke Bridge was swept away in a flood in 1818 and Ransomes were awarded the contract to replace it with an elegant iron one. Cubbitt originally conceived his treadmill as a cheap method of grinding corn with convict labour, but it was almost immediately adopted for simple penal purposes by every large prison in the country.

In the same year, the Ipswich Gas Light Company began supplying 150 taverns, shops and houses in the area between Carr Street and Cornhill. The plant, designed by Cubbitt and built and maintained by Ransomes, was at the southern corner of the foundry which now stretched down onto Carr Street itself.

Although the pressure was extremely low, the gas jets were said to be so resplendent that they almost obscured all neighbouring illuminations. The retail cost, which depended on the size of burner, was between £3 and £5 a year for unlimited use from dusk to 11pm or midnight. (Street lighting was charged at 21 shillings per lamp per annum, roughly cost price.) Consumers were on their honour not to light up outside contracted hours, an arrangement which worked satisfactorily with the respectable residents of the town centre. But when the system was enlarged in 1822 and new plant built by the river in St Clement's – another job for Ransomes – cheating became serious, and meters were introduced into suspect households.

By the 1820's, Ransomes had over 50 employees, and some of James's notes have survived about the more highly paid. *William Rush*: 'has now lived with us for 42 years ... one of our best and most faithful workmen ... His wages (31 shillings and 6 pence a week) have not been altered for a great many years.' (He wasn't doing too badly: prices almost halved in the decade after 1815.) *William Fletcher*: 'no danger of setting the Thames on fire'. *John Collins*: 'after engaging him I was disappointed ... Language highly offensive and his manners arbitrary and overbearing. The first he has corrected.' *Charles Clarke*: 'his irregularities from too much indulgence in drinking has occasioned our dealing very sharply with him and his wages had been much reduced in consequence (30 shillings to 24 shillings per week) ... His situation is improving.' *Nelson Sheppard*: 'it has been his usefulness in teaching others that has occasioned his having such high wages (28 shillings per week) which the slowness of his movements and lessening ability would hardly now entitle him to expect – but there is great difficulty in reducing the wages of old servants.'

The most cryptic entry refers to Stephen Keeble: 'this man was taken from the plough tail when he was scarcely up to his own in mud. The treasure we found in him no man can tell, and I believe no one but himself can guess at the extent of his genius . . . When he leaves us we may with truth say "We could better spare a better man".' We shall probably never know how much Ransomes, or indeed Ipswich, owes to this singular ploughman.

The railway boom of the 1830's and 40's brought a vast expansion to Ransomes' turnover which by 1851 had reached £122,000, £87,000 from this new technology. The number of employees rose to well over 1,000, around 1 in 7 of the town's male working population, and the business was moved in stages to the 10 acre site of the old St Clement's shipyards (now Orwell Quay), adjoining the new gas works. The firm's Mental Improvement Society started evening classes in the canteen there, which were well attended with sometimes 200 or 300 turning up. Agriculture began to revive, and the firm diversified into other implements than ploughshares, starting to produce its revolutionary lawnmower, at the rate of about 6 a month, in 1832. It was no more efficient than a scythe in the hands of a skilled gardener but it could be used, according to the advertisement, when the grass was wet.

In 1869, railway engineering was hived off into Ransome and Rapier as a totally separate company on the opposite bank of the river near Bayley's former yard in Stoke. It looks like the disposal of a division deemed to have gone ex-growth. However, perhaps contrary to expectations, it prospered.

By the century's end, the chimney stacks of the two Ransome companies and their neighbouring gas works were not the only ones to challenge the windmills and church towers on the town's skyline. Drawn in part by Ransomes' huge success and the skills and facilities it had created, other engineers arrived and developed into substantial enterprises, among the largest being E R & F Turner in 1837 by Wolsey's Gate, Cocksedge in 1879 at Greyfriars Road and Reavells in the 1890's opposite the railway station. Electricity was being generated in Carr Street before 1890, and there were several brick and cement works in St Helen's. By the mid-century, the mills by Handford and Stoke Bridges had been converted to coal.

As all this smoke drifted over the Tudor houses of the town centre, their spacious gardens were bought up and developed into the stinking alleys and courtyards of the workers' slums. Few old towns were destroyed so thoroughly; none with so distinguished a past.

CHAPTER FOURTEEN

The Poor

SLUMS were a Victorian phenomenon. The conditions of real poverty have always been horrendous, but the overcrowded and insanitary slum – the word first appears in an 1812 dictionary – struck a new chord in a society which by the 1830's had become convinced of the importance of both hygiene and reform. The former of course, by lowering the mortality rate, was largely responsible for the overcrowding, while the latter, reflecting the rising living standards and social awareness of the better-off, had made the whole problem appear ever more onerous to pocket and conscience alike.

Taking a long view, the percentage of the population regarded as paupers – a highly subjective judgement – had probably been falling slowly for centuries as the economy progressed. Nearly 20 per cent had availed themselves of Edward I's soup kitchen when he visited Ipswich for his daughter's wedding in 1297, and about 15 per cent had appeared on the parish poor lists in 1597. The official figure for 1835 was 2,300 or 10 per cent.

Anything like that number may well have represented an improving percentage, but to the comfortable burgesses of Ipswich in 1800 it was probably more daunting as a screaming mob than 600 unruly peasants would have seemed to the tougher contemporaries of Edward I.

One Saturday that autumn, following a poor harvest and seven inflationary years of war, a hungry horde ransacked the food stalls and shops round Cornhill. Next week they were prudently kept closed, and the crowd turned its attention to the tide mill at Stoke Bridge. The volunteer Ipswich Regiment was called out for its first serious engagement while brave Mr Batley, the Town Clerk, read out the relevant sentence of the Riot Act. In the exhilarating battle with bags of flour which ensued inside the warehouse, all thoughts of sneaking the stuff home were forgotten. When the soldiers got the upper hand, the crowd beat a strategic retreat to St Peter's churchyard where for some reason stones and bricks were plentiful. Thence they were dispersed by a cavalry charge down St Peter's Street ordered from St Matthew's barracks. Remarkably, there was no bloodshed; but it no doubt concentrated the minds of the many critics of the poor rate.

It was 230 years since £170 had been raised from the parishes as a poor rate to finance Christ's Hospital. That establishment, some time after the last of the Elizabethan Poor Laws in 1601, had given up its role as the municipal workhouse and become a school. In the sixteenth century, most people had paid a rate of between 4 and 8 shillings a year. It was not – on average – so different in 1800, in real terms over 50 per cent less.

The average, however, was very misleading. After 1601 each parish became entirely responsible for its own poor. The poorer the parish, therefore the greater the expense. The wealthier parishes like St Lawrence's, St Stephen's and St Mary le Tower in the town centre, where there were few paupers, paid relatively little, although it was the richest residents who complained the loudest. In 1822 an influential committee published a pamphlet to show that as a result of bad management the parishes of Ipswich were spending on the poor several times as much per head as those in towns such as Plymouth, Bristol and Lincoln, or even in rural Suffolk. Perhaps Ipswich was more caring, but the committee never considered that.

Over the years the Ipswich parishes had received numerous bequests to provide the poor with food and warmth. By 1800 the aggregate income from this source was around £400 a year, over a quarter for St Mary Elms via Ann Smyth's charity. Each parish was required by law to keep a poor house for desperate cases, and many such houses were bequests also. The effect of all this in practice was to reduce the rates burden on the paupers' more affluent neighbours, hardly what the original benefactors had envisaged.

Mrs Ann Smyth's rather complicated will of 1729 provided for her money to be administered by the London Drapers' Company who, perhaps fearing trouble with the family, refused to accept the trust. The curates of St Peter's and St Mary Elms were appointed instead. After a £2,000 legacy to a grandson or, in certain circumstances, a nephew, she bequeathed the remainder (£5,000 or £6,000 as she thought, although the net sum was £4,432) to build and maintain an almshouse in St Mary Elms for twelve poor women over 50 years of age. Priority was to be given to certain of her own relations. They must all be communicants of the Church of England, and attend a service every Wednesday and Friday at St Mary Elms, for which the Parson would receive £10 a year.

The burden on the parishes was further reduced to the extent of £1,500 a year by two charities run by the Corporation, the Tooley and Smart Foundations (the latter set up under the will of the Town Library's founder) which now supported, either in the Foundation Street almshouses or their own homes, about 130 old people. (Tooley's five original almshouses had been replaced and increased in number after his foundation had been linked with Smart's in the seventeenth century. The present buildings were put up on a site nearby in 1846.)

The thinking behind the researches of the 1822 committee was that the parish overseers were a soft touch. Many an able-bodied pauper receiving relief at home was as well off as his employed neighbour, and it was felt he ought to earn his dole. If he couldn't or – as was thought more likely – wouldn't find work, it should be provided compulsorily at his poor house which was then catering chiefly for the young, the sick and the aged.

The poor houses were often called workhouses, and it had always been intended that paupers should contribute towards their keep, but only in St Clement's, which had 23 residents in 1835, is there any evidence of work (spinning) being undertaken. They were paid 5 pence pocket money out of every 18 pence earned, which could take some time.

Poorhouse meals consisted of bread and cheese every day for lunch, and meat, gravy and suet pudding for supper – hot for three days a week and cold for three. On Monday, supper, like lunch, was bread and cheese. Beer was normally provided, and the staff in theory had the same food as their charges. The cost was reckoned to average up to 3 shillings per week per pauper, or a total for the whole town of about £1,600 a year. The poor houses, whose capacity is unlikely to have exceeded 250, gave indoor relief: outdoor relief, supplied in their own homes to everyone else thought to be in need, worked out at almost the same amount per head.

In modern purchasing power, as an extremely rough guide and based on figures which are themselves approximations, it looks as if in 1297 – for just a fortnight – the poor received the equivalent of £20 a week per head, in 1597 under £1 a week, and in 1800 £10. Pensioners of the Tooley and Smart charities in the latter year were getting £12 a week each, plus in a number of cases accommodation, worth as much again today.

Relief arrangements were reorganised in 1835 to comply with the new Poor Act. Three Relieving Officers replaced the parochial overseers and most of the old poor houses were shut. Their inmates, then totalling 176, were divided among the three largest: St Margaret's for women and girls, St Clement's for men and boys and St Mary le Tower's for the aged and infirm. The men were set to pick oakum or make rush matting, the boys to mend shoes, and the women and girls to knit. Nobody now was paid. The changes were not popular, possibly the vestries stirred up trouble, and riots outside St Margaret's and St Clement's had to be broken up by troops.

Two years later, the Ipswich Union Workhouse, purpose-built to

The Wet Dock and New Cut from the Workhouse garden.

hold 400, was opened in Stoke between Great Whip Street and the river, and everyone from the three houses was transferred there.

By then the East Suffolk and Ipswich Hospital for the sick poor had been in operation for a full year from its beautiful site at the top of Berners Street. On the initiative of Dykes Alexander £5,000 (double what was needed for the building) was raised in no time. Interest from the surplus, plus legacies and annual subscriptions gave it an income of £1,000 a year, plenty in the early years because with 50 beds it was seldom full. Except in emergencies, admittance was on the recommendation of a subscriber.

For purposes of economy and to discourage the supposedly work-shy, the workhouse meat ration was reduced by one-third, the bulk being made up of more bread and roots. Gravy and beer were stopped altogether. (On the other hand, for a short period, until the Assistant Commissioner got to hear about it, children and elderly were allowed to receive sweets and fruit from visitors.) A schoolmaster and mistress were introduced, despite qualms that the children, taught to write as well as read, might gain an unfair advantage over those outside. And in an advertising campaign, help was offered to emigrants to America or the North of England where jobs were alleged to be more plentiful.

Despite this propaganda, the number of inmates rose in 1838 to 289. There were as many as 509 admittances in that year because not a few able-bodied tramps and others were sent to the workhouse for a short, sharp shock. Work, which included breaking a quota of stones or picking 1lb of oakum before breakfast, was provided for everyone who was not suffering from constipation, bruising, quinsey, hysteria, abscesses, bad legs, bad fingers or any of the other recorded ailments which might offer brief exemption. 'You're better off in a pig sty', said one man, 'the pigs treat you kinder'.

The indoor relief of the new Workhouse doubtlessly did produce economies, but the real savings were achieved in the operation of out-relief. In 1834, under the old regime, the total cost of both forms of relief had been over £15,000. By 1840 it was £13,000 and by 1850 £12,000, in spite of a 50 per cent increase in the population since 1834, and 75 per cent in the numbers seeking help. Clearly this was not accomplished by efficiency alone: out-relief on average per head was halved, and everyone suffered, deserving and undeserving alike.

The neat copperplate of the Relieving Officers' dispassionate reports makes grim reading. James and Lucy Wade with their seven children, one of whom was deaf and dumb, received 3 shillings and 6 pence a week, plus 28lbs of flour, worth as much again. The family had no furniture of any kind and the children slept on straw thinly scattered across the floor. Wade was soon afterwards imprisoned for debt, and Lucy, a charwoman, moved out of the parish. Samuel Tydeman was a constant terror to his wife and two children: he had given up a good job to become a peddler, and was awarded no relief but loaned a pound. George Page also got nothing: 'a most depraved character, drunken and insolent and uses his wife brutally'. Thomas Matt, another peddler, 'sometimes employed with his violin', received 14lbs of flour for his family of eight. Thomas Stannard had a wife and two children in great destitution: it was 'absolutely necessary' to supply them with blankets as well as 28lbs of flour. George Spinkes, aged 70, whose wife had just died, got nothing because his grown-up children were capable of supporting him.

Many men are dismissed as 'habitual drunkard' or 'very troublesome' and seldom got anything; (if they were able-bodied that was the law now). Some, without the option, like the failed pimp, Robert Barham, were sent to the workhouse. A few were 'offered' it. The plight of Daniel Haggar, a consumptive, produces a rare sparklet of sympathy: 'he suffered great deprivation before he would apply – a deserving case'. He got 2 shillings a week and 28lbs of flour.

Widows and unmarried mothers now far outnumbered the men. Sarah Rogers was a cook at The Great White Horse: she employed another woman to look after her 5 small children after her husband's death, and was given 2 shillings plus 28lbs of flour. Eliza Lamb, aged 68, who had several prostitute daughters, one of whom was receiving relief for two bastards, was sent to the workhouse. Maria Juby, abusive and violent, an obvious troublemaker, was left to starve. The widowed Susan Glading, aged 60, had to dispose of her dog before she was found room in the workhouse. Sarah Smith, discovered sick and penniless in St Nicholas Street, was given a shilling to get out of town. Mary Lee, whose sailor husband earned 10 shillings a week, was provided with a daily pint of beer for her health. And, although the workhouse took in lunatics, and there was a Union asylum off the Woodbridge Road called Belle Vue, Charlotte Borrett, 'wholly insane', was sent to the one at Melton.

As the years passed, one has the impression that the Relieving Officers' concern to distribute their limited resources as fairly as possible began to wane. They had seen it all before. And how can you calibrate desperation in pennies? Laconic epithets like 'sick', destitute', or 'homeless' replace their earlier sober vignettes; and relief, which previously had varied widely between one shilling and seven, became almost stereotyped around 2 shillings – punctuated from time to time by a final and explicit 30 shillings: 'coffin and fees'.

During the 1870's up to 235 workhouse children – initially not all from the Ipswich Union – were resettled at St John's Home in California, exchanging the adult jungle of one institution for another probably no less vicious of their own.

In 1899, after 30 years of prodding by the Poor Commission, an expensive new workhouse was opened at the top of the Woodbridge Road to replace the crumbling old one in Stoke. It was designed with 'special regard' for the comfort of the sick and elderly. The rest of the residents – the capacity of the house was around 500, now financed by a fairer apportionment between the parishes – were almost by definition deemed lazy, or at best immoral.

With this in mind, a points' system was worked out. Class I, the well-behaved over 65, were allowed 1½ ozs of tobacco a week or (for the women) 2½ ozs of tea and ½ lb of sugar, together with cake on Sunday and an egg and butter on Friday. Class II, the fairly well-behaved over 65, got 1 oz of tobacco, or 2 ozs of tea and ½ lb of sugar, plus an egg on Friday. Class III, everyone else, including the badly-behaved over 65, had none of these treats. All, however, had treacle with their pudding on Monday and cocoa instead of tea for supper on Friday.

Pandering to the stirring sensibilities of the twentieth century, the name Union Workshouse was dropped in favour of Heathfields. The Union itself was abolished in 1929 when poverty was made the responsibility of the Corporation's Public Health Department. The workhouse continued as an Old People's Home and was replaced in the 1970's by the Heath Road Hospital.

Conditions in the workhouse did not differ markedly from those in prison, and indeed it was sometimes called the Bastille. Unlike prison, you could of course get out, either on one of the regular exeat days, or permanently if your circumstances changed, perhaps through a relation's kindness or a miracle. (Even at Heathfields, less rigorous than the old Stoke workhouse, exeats were strictly controlled, from once a week to once a month, depending on which Class you were in.)

The County Jail had been in Falcon Street until 1718 when for the next 68 years parts of the jails in the Westgate and Black Horse Lane were shared with the town. Then the County built another of its own in St Helen's. The Town Jails were far from secure and difficult prisoners had to be housed elsewhere. The new jail (the one from which Margaret Catchpole escaped) was a model of its kind, with corridors radiating from a central hub, a courtyard garden and the latest sanitary devices. Men and women were kept apart, and smugglers and debtors were held separately from the real criminals. Naturally it was one of the first to purchase a treadmill from Ransomes.

The grim Westgate Jail was demolished in 1781 and, after the one in Black Horse Lane had suffered a similar fate, the Town Jail was itself transferred in the 1820's to the former House of Correction, also in St Helen's. This institution had been originally set up as a tough work-

Inspector Edmonds on duty.

house for tramps and troublemakers with whom the parish overseers were unable to cope in their poor houses.

Constables, elected annually by the parish vestries, had for centuries been responsible for maintaining law and order. Their place was taken in 1836 by 15 of the new Police variety, under the command of 3 Inspectors. The troops of the garrison resented these fresh uniformed rivals (uniforms were worn at all times) who often went out of their way to be officious, especially if a soldier was accompanied by a girl: her name, address and occupation were demanded and a close scrutiny made of her bonneted face. The case of Trooper Flinn, beaten up by Inspector Edmonds and another officer was eventually referred to the Home Secretary who on rather scanty evidence exonerated them.

The Ipswich crime rate, which had been accelerating for thirty years before the Force's formation, continued to do so afterwards. The Chief Constable blandly ascribed this to an improved detection rate. To be fair, it was a nationwide trend, reflecting the growing gap between wealth and poverty.

About a quarter of the early recruits had been labourers, so Police pay of between 14 and 17 shillings a week, supplemented by various fees taken over from their parochial predecessors was rather more than they had been accustomed to. They spent the extra money in many cases on drink. Almost half the police in East Suffolk in the first twenty-five years were dismissed either for actually being drunk on duty or for being absent from the beat – when they may well have been drinking. Robert Harvey, a tailor of St Margaret's Green, was one of the first to join the force in 1836, replacing a senior constable who had been caught on duty in a tavern with a couple of girls. During a brief career, Harvey himself was reported both for illegally soliciting Christmas boxes and for attacking a woman. He in turn reported Edmonds and another Inspector for introducing prostitutes into the Police House. They were dismissed for that, and then reinstated. Harvey was advised to resign for health reasons.

Pay was better and the work easier in the rural Constabularies, and there was much scheming among the Ipswich police to move to the country. The Watch Committee remained convinced, however, that the Borough's force was second to none, and they may have been right.

Police numbers, already inadequate for a town the size of Ipswich, were reduced to 10 in 1844 as a result of ratepayer objections that the whole new apparatus was too expensive. Six Specials, paid 4 shillings a day, were put on stand-by, a poor exchange which was soon reversed.

The Shire Hall.

By 1890, when top hats had been replaced by helmets, the town's regular police totalled sixty and a senior Constable was earning nearly 26 shillings a week.

The town had always maintained the independence of its Portmansmote and other Courts from Sheriff and county. County Quarter Sessions and Assizes were sometimes held here rather than at Bury, and in 1699 the Shire Hall was built in the Blackfriars precinct to encourage their presence which was good for trade. That did not entirely succeed because the judges were better entertained at Bury.

The Shire Hall was abandoned in 1837 and replaced – coincidentally rather in the style of the Bastille – by a building in St Helen's Street in front of the County Jail. There were useful facilities for executions on the roof of the gatekeeper's lodge. It achieved international renown in 1936 when Mrs Simpson obtained her divorce there, and remains the County Hall today.

CHAPTER FIFTEEN

River and Rail

STOWMARKET during the seventeenth century had ambitions to replace Ipswich as the county town. In some ways, Assizes or no Assizes, it was more of a threat than clerical and gentrified Bury. More centrally located than either of them, it was already the place where a number of county events were held and, with barely 1,000 inhabitants, afforded an emptier site than cluttered-up Ipswich for the fashionable practitioners of town planning. It would also be more convenient for the farmers who sent their produce by sea to London, provided the Gipping could be made navigable.

In 1719 plans were afoot to do just that; but the Ipswich Council, understandably fearful that, at the nadir of the town's commercial fortunes, a booming Stowmarket only 16 miles upstream might spell the port's final ruin, successfully opposed the idea. By 1790, however, when the whole country had been criss-crossed by profitable canals, the animal spirits of the Ipswich merchants, with increasing trade and population, began to reassert themselves. And the possible risks to the community posed by the construction of the Gipping Navigation seemed well compensated by its prospective rewards to a private investor of a heady 10 per cent.

In the event, as so often happens, this risk/reward ratio turned out to be less dramatic: investors received nearer 6 per cent than 10 after costs of straightening bits of the river and building 15 locks exceeded the £25,000 estimate by half as much again; while, partly thanks to Napoleon's declaration of war 7 months before the Navigation's opening, the turnover of the port of Ipswich suffered no perceptible damage. Even so, one of the incidental advantages of the subsequent West Dock scheme of 1835 was deemed to be that it would make life more difficult for users of the Gipping Navigation.

More than anything else, this great scheme for a Wet Dock, which took a generation to mature, symbolises the renaissance of Ipswich. Both Tooley and Smart had left small sums of money to help dredge

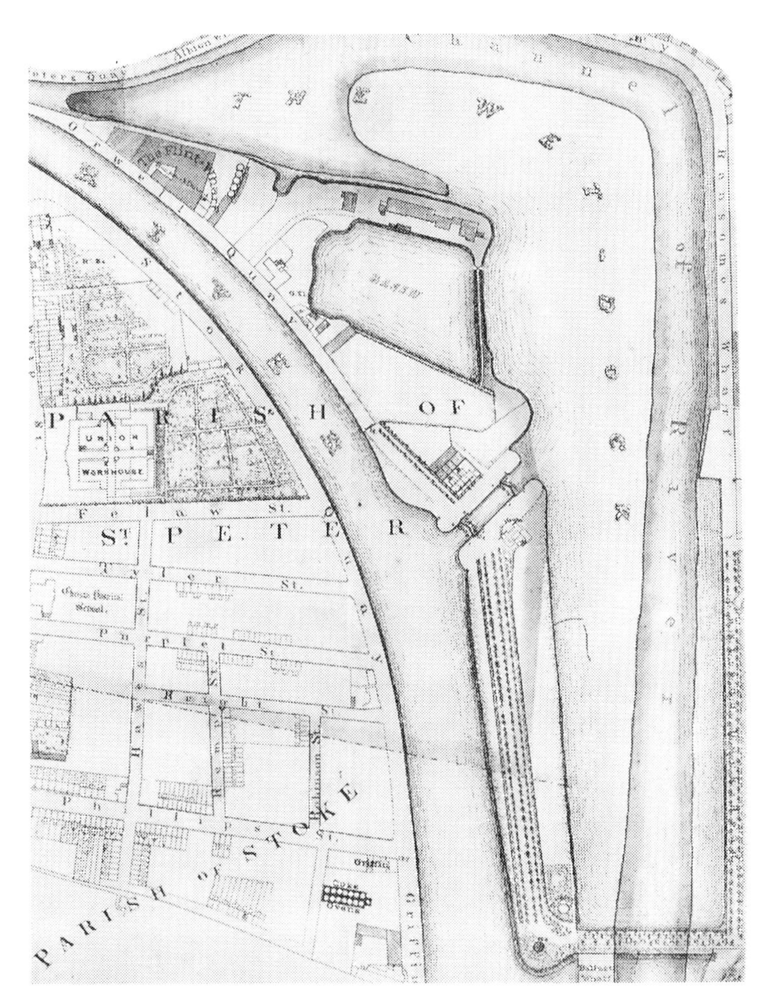

Plan of the Wet Dock.

the Orwell, but if anything was done, it was not effective. Long before 1797 the Common Quay had become inaccessible to all but the smallest vessels and, as had been necessary on occasions in Tooley's day, most cargo had regularly to be trans-shipped at Downham Reach near the modern Orwell Bridge.

In that year a Subscribers' Committee was formed to consider the options: either to build a separate canal from Downham Reach leading to a wet dock behind a barrage just east of the Common Quay or, more cheaply, merely to dredge the mud near the quay and deepen and straighten the three worst bends of the river's channel as far as Downham.

The Town Council, which was not represented on this committee and set up a rival one of its own, produced a plan to borrow the cash required on the security of temporarily increased import and tonnage duties and to control the whole operation itself. The subscribers, the potential source of all the money, wisely vetoed it. As someone pointed out with heavy humour, although the Council was rightfully the guardian of the soil of Ipswich, it had already failed in its duty by leaving so much of it at the bottom of the Orwell.

Discussion continued for eight years until an Act of Parliament transformed the Subscribers' Committee into a River Commission of 72 members with full powers independent of the Council. Its unwieldy size was necessary probably because raising the money was not easy. Certainly, against professional advice, the cheaper alternative costing £15,000 was chosen. This would enable ships of 250 tons to enter the port in favourable conditions provided the channel was kept dredged, an additional recurring expense.

An initial tranche of £8,000 was subscribed of which £2,000 was spent on drafting the Act and £3,000 on purchasing a steam dredger. In theory, its operating cost per ton was half that of the manual labour, the Mud Men, who were also used. When the dredger was not laid up for repairs, sometimes for months on end, it could shift nearly 100 tons

The new Customs House.

of spoil a day which was either kept for sale as ballast if it was sand or gravel, or dumped downstream.

The project was completed before 1830. Duties produced around £2,500 a year, and this had been more than enough to fund annual expenditure once the original £8,000 was spent. Having repaid that, the Commissioners had a surplus of £25,000 which, unless they could think of something to do with it, they would be obliged under the Act to leave invested in 3 per cent government bonds and use the income for the river's maintenance in place of the import duties. Needless to say, they thought of something.

The old wet dock scheme, minus the canal, was resurrected. The barrage was to be further downstream than before, below the Gas Works, creating a vast tideless dock of 32 acres, three times the size of the earlier plan and greater than anything in London. The New Cut, dredged from the mud along the Stoke shore, and separated from the dock by a thin 14-acre 'island', would allow the river's flow to by-pass the dock, while the latter's single entrance lock would be half way up the Cut, more sheltered in rough weather than an opening lower downstream in the barrage.

The management of the Gipping Navigation offered to pay for a second entrance at Stoke Bridge for ships coming down to Ipswich. Otherwise they would have to sail down the full length of the Cut and turn back to the dock entrance which was angled to face downstream, thereby losing a tide. The offer was rejected.

Just in time for the railway construction boom, the Wet Dock, financed and run by the new Dock Commission, 107 strong, opened in 1842. The port's income, now from tonnage and coal duty only, doubled in the first full year thereafter. It was just as well it did, for building costs too had doubled to about £130,000, so that the Commission's £5,000 revenue was barely sufficient to service borrowings, even allowing for the £25,000 endowment from its predecessor.

Since the collapse of its cloth exports, Ipswich trade has been overwhelmingly coastal and, contrary to expectations that the new dock would gain much overseas business at the expense of Harwich, or even London, it remained so. In the 1830's, less than one foreign ship a week was using Ipswich: in the 1850's when the Commission's income had doubled again, it was two a week. That compares with 30 coastal vessels a week in 1855, many of course bringing coal and pig iron in rapidly increasing quantities to Ransomes and others, and taking away ploughshares, rail parts, lawnmowers and machinery.

The whole length of the town-side waterfront was widened by an

The Promenade.

embankment so that, perhaps for the first time since the days that the Bigots, Harneys and the like had set up their wharves there, it was possible to walk all the way from St Peter's to St Clement's along the river. The Corporation spent £4,000 which it could ill afford on knocking down the Customs House, old in Tooley's time, and putting up the present one, a confident, monumental building which exactly expressed the town's new mood.

Beyond the Gas Works, the furthest section of the embankment (later called Helena Road after the floating sailor's church on the Helena moored nearby) became a tree-lined avenue leading to a wide path across the barrage and onto the strip of land which separated the dock from the New Cut. Here a Promenade was laid out, shaded by three rows of limes and poplars, and furnished with seats plus a bandstand known as The Umbrella. Pegasus, the winged horse, the Ipswich equivalent to the Statue of Liberty, looked across on the passing traffic. The Promenade stretched up as far as the dock gates. On their other side, beyond the lock keepers' cottages, were more trees and a small artificial stone works with its tide mill. An agreeable scene,

Pegasus and the Umbrella.

blighted by the twentieth century, but surely not impossible to restore in the twenty-first.

Soon the size and angle of the entrance lock, awkwardly placed and only 140 feet long, became too tight for the growing number of larger ships. During the five years to 1874, the port's revenue fell by one-third. A new 300 foot lock was proposed in the barrage at the southern end facing the estuary, always the obvious place provided an extra pair of outer gates were fitted as a protection against exceptional tides.

The Commissioners were reluctant. More construction meant more duties to pay for it, and that didn't suit their private interests, still exclusively concerned with the ownership of small coastal vessels. But the opposition persisted, led by an important newcomer to the town, the East Anglian Daily Times (which well described the Commissioners as a heterogeneous mob of Rip Van Winkles) and in 1881 the new lock was opened. 'The Liverpool of the East Coast', said the newspaper. The old entrance was filled in later; but the emergency additional gates were considered an unnecessary expense, a decision which continued to be justified until they were finally erected in 1976.

June 11th 1846 was a public holiday in Ipswich, ordained by the Mayor to celebrate the opening of the railway.

At 10.30am the train left Halifax Junction near the Stoke Green Baptist chapel and arrived at Colchester at 11.45. (The tunnel under Stoke Hill was not finished, and it would be another 14 years before funds were available to build the present station on its town side.) The twelve carriages, full of shareholders, directors and other prominent personages, plus a truck for the band, were seen off by the 600 fluttering handkerchiefs of their wives, daughters and others for whom a stand had been erected. The company's chairman, John Chevallier Cobbold, the eldest of the 14 children of John Cobbold the younger, with a fine sense of the dramatic, joined the train amid cheering crowds and passengers half-way down the line at Bentley. Possibly that was the reason why the journey took so long: they all got back to Ipswich in under an hour, in time for lunch in or beside the train shed with their patient womenfolk.

That evening, a gala dinner at the Assembly Room for the top brass, and at the Golden Lion and the Coach and Horses for others, was followed by fireworks over the new dock. The Assembly Room dinner started at 5 o'clock, so the diners would have missed the 6.30 balloon ascent from the Grammar School playground. The navvies who were still working on the tunnel, were entertained more simply at the Railroad Tavern on Stoke Hill. They were a rowdy lot, unlike their mates who had been building the track, and at the Rector's insistence, were supervised by a policeman.

For Cobbold, a solicitor, now in his fiftieth year, it was the culmination of a ten-years' struggle to bring the railway to Ipswich. In 1836 the Eastern Counties Railway had obtained the necessary Act of Parliament to build a line from London via Ipswich and Norwich to Yarmouth, 126 miles, the largest single enterprise of its kind so far undertaken. Apart from the Cobbolds, few people in East Anglia were interested, and almost 90 per cent of the shares were subscribed in Liverpool and Birmingham where the railways had already made an impact. Half the directors were local men, and half from London, the Midlands and Lancashire.

The combination of northern brass, concerned exclusively with profit, and the laid-back attitude of the East Anglians, who simply wanted a nice railway and as high a price as possible for the land it would go through, was not a happy one. The northerners, having left responsibility for land purchases to the local directors, realised their

John Chevallier Cobbold.

mistake too late, and by the time the railway had reached Colchester in 1843, money was running out.

After a series of boardroom battles, most of the locals were sacked including Cobbold's aged father and uncle. (The latter, Dr Chevallier, Squire and Parson of Aspall, like so many clergymen, was a railway enthusiast: 18 years earlier, even before the Rocket had introduced the new era, he had chaired an abortive committee to construct a line from Ipswich to Diss, incidentally passing across his own land.)

It was clear by now that the Eastern Counties were not keen to continue their line beyond Colchester. At a shareholders' meeting, Cobbold the solicitor, who was not a director, after threatening to ask Parliament to compel the company to raise more money to do so, proposed that with what was left they should at once buy up all the

The station at Halifax Junction.

land needed as far as Ipswich. A director asked if this idea had anything to do with Cobbold's purchase, within days of the original Act being passed, of the Crane Hall estate astride the London Road which was directly on the line's planned route. He replied that he had at the time offered the property to the company, and at cost. It was confirmed that the offer had certainly been made, but nobody could remember anything being said about cost.

Cobbold soon obtained another Act for a totally new company, the Eastern Union, to complete the missing link to Ipswich. He engaged Peter Bruff as the railway's engineer, a talented young man who had just been sacked by the Eastern Counties for carelessness. (His father, he said, had been a Royal Naval Captain and a friend of Nelson. Here too he was careless: people knew all about Nelson in Ipswich, and it soon came out that Bruff senior, a warrant officer, had probably never even spoken to Nelson.)

Bruff calculated the capital required for a line on a more easterly route than the original plan was only £200,000 (a quarter of the Eastern Counties' estimate) which, on what were considered rather optimistic forecasts, would produce a dividend of 7½per cent. A good and reliable stream of bulk freight was – and is – essential to maximise a line's profitability, typically moving goods from port to inland centre, and the Eastern Union would simply connect two ports. Moreover, as against existing stage-coach numbers, passenger traffic was expected to double, a reasonable assumption, but not convincing to the monied classes of Ipswich who seemed quite satisfied with the twice-daily Quicksilver coach service between the Coach and Horses in Upper

Proposed tunnel entrance under Stoke Hill.

Brook Street and Colchester Station. In the end, most of the cash was put up by the directors, plus the many members of the Cobbold clan, and a few stray investors in Huddersfield.

The task of buying the land was left to Cobbold's vice-chairman, the draper John Footman, the largest shopkeeper in town whom everybody trusted. The construction was undertaken by one man on a fixed price contract employing a multitude of small contractors each responsible for a mile or so of line who in turn often sub-contracted to independent gangs about a dozen strong. There were around 1,000 men in all, mostly quite local, who either lodged in adjacent villages or in huts beside the workings. They operated in shifts, day and night. That included Sundays until after a public outcry the Mayor visited the sites himself and forbade it. There were 10 fatalities altogether, three of them in the tunnel at Stoke, a remarkably low figure considering the hazards of night working by lantern light.

The tunnel, on a sharp curve never previously attempted, was actually built by the Eastern Union's sister company, the Bury and Ipswich, which the determined Cobbold had formed to provide a link from Halifax Junction via Crane Hall land to Bury and Norwich.

Commencement and completion of the excavations under Stoke Hill were marked with suitable ceremony. The Mayor, dressed like a navvy with a cotton band round his head, filled the first barrow and wheeled it to the dumping site; and a year later, three months after the Colchester line was opened, the directors assembled again to insert the four final bricks into the tunnel wall. One recorded the date, and the others bore the names of Cobbold, Footman and Bruff. Footman wore gloves to deal with his, a cause of much ribaldry.

Lack of money meant that the proposed grand portals of the tunnel entrances had to be reduced to the utilitarian entrances seen today, although Bury, Stowmarket and Needham Market, thanks to local pressure, got their fine stations as planned. Needham Market's, a rare example of Mr Barnes's Elizabethan style, now barely recognisable, cost the large sum of £3,150. Bury station was the better of the two designs short-listed for Ipswich where the platforms at Halifax Junction were considered good enough for the time being.

Single fares to London for the three classes of carriage were 15 shillings, 10 shillings, and 5 shillings and 8 pence. The first class had windows and upholstered seats, the second class seats were leather-covered, and the third class, with a roof but partly open sides, had wooden seats. Originally the second class too had wooden seats, and the leather was added to attract the better-off who were tending to travel third class, despite notices that third was 'For the Working Classes'. There was also a fourth class, half the price of third, which applied to standing or squatting in goods wagons when available. Perhaps appropriately, that rate approximates in real terms to the present second class fare.

The Eastern Union took over the Bury and Ipswich Railway soon after the line to Bury was finished in December 1846. A branch track was also built across the Gipping and along the new quays via a shunting and goods yard south of Commercial Road. The waste land adjoining was acquired by Cobbold and Footman on their personal account. That investment took time to mature. The railway had contracted in 1845 to build Princes Street and Bridge to link the station with Cornhill, as well as Portman Road to link it with St Matthew's. They were little more than dangerous tracks, however, when the station was finally opened in 1860. Cobbold offered to finance part of the road construction himself, which would have enhanced the value of his adjacent land, but in the end the job was completed by the railway.

The combined company, with a capital approaching £2m. and

debts of £1m., was now a substantial operation. John Footman resigned as managing director in March 1849. Bruff, the engineer, took over his job, not the ideal choice. Cobbold was an ideas man while his remaining co-directors, some of whom ran successful businesses of their own though on a smaller scale, seem to have been overawed by the strength of their chairman's personality and the length of his purse and pedigree. Running costs, reckoned to be about 40 per cent of revenue for a healthy railway, reached 50 per cent by 1850 and a critical 60 per cent in 1853, despite redundancies and pay cuts for the staff, and the waiving of fees by the directors. Staff cuts saved £3,000 and directors' fees £14,000.

Even so, Cobbold persisted with work on the Bury-Norwich line which was completed by the New Year of 1850. That may have been the reason for Footman's resignation because it brought the Eastern Union at once into an inevitable clash with the Eastern Counties which already had a Norwich line via Cambridge.

Relations between the two companies had never been easy where their 7 each-way trains a day met head-on at Colchester. London passengers always had to change there, walking the length of its long

Peter Bruff in middle age.

platforms (the longest in England) between the connecting trains. In no circumstances was Eastern Union rolling stock permitted to trespass one inch into Eastern Counties territory.

The journey between Ipswich and London normally took three hours: after battle was joined over the Norwich routes, it was nearer four hours, if you were lucky. Eastern Counties altered its timetables to make Colchester connections as awkward as possible, its ticket clerks and inspectors in London affected never to have heard of Ipswich, and fares were increased on the Colchester to London line by 18 per cent, and reduced to Norwich. Cobbold told the story of a friend of his who about this time received an unexpected case of champagne by rail from London. They opened it together only to find it was a repackaged consignment of castor oil.

Belatedly after a year of harassment, the Eastern Union directors used their powers under the Act to refer the dispute to arbitration. Then, as it became apparent the opposition would drag out the inquiry for at least 18 months, they experimented with a competing steamer service daily each way between Ipswich and London with connecting trains. From quay to quay the sea journey in good weather couldn't have taken much less than seven hours but it was advertised as taking four. Five ships were purchased, mostly with Cobbold cash. Prices were set well below the rail equivalent, and the operation, which only lasted a year, can never have been profitable after financing and setting-up costs. It was Cobbold's last throw of the dice: it would hurt his own company but he evidently imagined it would harm his powerful opponents even more.

By the time the arbitrators had pronounced in favour of the Eastern Union, the company was insolvent. On January 1st 1854, after an inglorious life of barely eight years, its running was taken over by the Eastern Counties. In a further eight, with passengers no longer having to change at Colchester, the companies were formally merged as the Great Eastern.

The Gipping Navigation was leased to the Bury and Ipswich Railway in 1846. Traffic, as expected, fell 75 per cent but, as little was spent on maintenance, income at first just about covered costs. The main users now were the fertiliser manufacturers: Prentices exporting their products from Stowmarket, and Packards transporting coprolite up from Ipswich to their plant at Bramford.

Coprolite, which means fossilised dung, is a pebble-like substance, rich in phosphate, whose merits are reputed to have been discovered by a Levington farmer around 1700. Local deposits had just started to be exploited commercially. They were exhausted by 1860 and were replaced by imports from North Africa.

Packards' mill was by the quay in St Clement's, between what is now Coprolite Street and Ransomes' new Orwell Works. Originally the coprolite had been processed in the mill, crushed and then dissolved in sulphuric acid, but the smell was so bad that the operation had to be moved to Bramford, leaving the site for offices and warehousing. Nearby were the town's Turkish Baths.

By 1888 when the railway's lease expired, the Gipping had become almost unnavigable above Bramford. The black funnels of Packards' barges were now competing with the white funnels of another company beside Stoke Bridge, the flour and fertiliser millers, Joseph Fison & Co. A high tide was needed to reach Bramford, but not too high because, even with funnels lowered, the barges were a tight fit under the single span of Cubbitt's bridge. Once, a steam safety valve was damaged and the skipper was scalded to death. Sometimes the river froze over and iron thumpers were used to break the ice. In 1895 traffic of another kind took over when for 16 weeks it was possible to traverse the river's entire length to Stowmarket on skates.

The three fertiliser businesses merged in 1929 as Fison, Packard and Prentice Ltd, and the Navigation with assets of £216 closed for good.

Wet Dock from the big gas holder, 1938.

CHAPTER SIXTEEN

The Schools

HAIR-POWDER was taxed in 1795, a Tory measure to help pay for the war against Napoleon. It was an annual 21 shillings literally per head. Prices were beginning to rise, and many people gave up using it to save money and, depending on their political persuasion, to spite the government.

Now, John King, the Town Preacher and Headmaster of Ipswich School, always wore a wig. A barber came each week before school to dress it. Would he continue to have it powdered? No one knew his politics, and speculation among the boys was intense.

The grammar schoolroom at Blackfriars, 1768–1843.

On the crucial morning, the schoolroom's two windows overlooking the old Blackfriars' cloister were crowded. The barber arrived, punctual to the minute, and crossed to the Headmaster's room. Soon the bell rang for the start of school. Silence, and the heavy clanging of the school keys as Mr King removed their thong from its peg in his study. The door opened . . . no powder.

Before his arrival thirty years earlier, the school had been housed in the old Clothworkers' Hall next to the Town Library in the Blackfriars' former dormitory. It had recently been moved thither from the friars' refectory on the opposite side of the cloister. This building, running beside Foundation Street, was on land with development potential and was knocked down. (Before that of course, until 1612, the school had been in Felaw's house opposite.)

There cannot have been room for more than about 60 boys in the Clothworkers' Hall, and Mr King, who turned out to be one of the school's more effective Headmasters, probably made its enlargement a condition of his taking the post. The Town Library was moved downstairs to the damp old sacristy (the dormitory was on the first floor) and the adjoining gunpowder store was relocated a healthier distance away in Christ's Hospital. Thus with partitions removed, the dormitory was restored to it full length, doubling the school's space.

The Headmaster's house had originally been situated next to Felaw's in Foundation Street, but by 1705 this had been given to the Guider or Warden of Christ's Hospital. It was now on the east side of Lower Brook Street, in the Town Preacher's residence whose large garden backed onto Foundation Street and provided easy access to Blackfriars. Here Mr King took in up to 70 boarders (far more than any of his predecessors) mostly two to a bed.

Bullying was common, as in most schools. The boys played cricket in the garden, flew kites and grew vegetables. They mimicked the writing-master who had trouble with his aitches, 'putting them in and leaving them out in the wrong places'. They stole the neighbours' fruit and played with gunpowder – evidently as easily available to small boys as cigarettes today – for which they were beaten if caught. Mr King and his assistant master always carried a stick for the purpose. Most beatings were for poor results in class. Cooper, one of the thickest boys of his year, usually had to bend over two or three times a week. Day boys' truancy was similarly punished, perhaps less effectively then a penny fine formerly imposed on their parents by the 1571 Ordinances of the Great Court.

These Ordinances, modified over the years, were quite specific.

The school was to hold no more than 112 boys in 7 forms, and only twelve could be boarders. Preference must be given to the sons of freemen provided they could read and write. School hours, during which only Latin might be spoken, were from 7–11am and 1–4pm 6 days a week except for a half holiday on Thursday. Once a week the whole school must attend a sermon in church, and selected boys (no doubt informed afterwards) write an essay about it on their return to school. After the Gunpowder Plot, the Head Boy had to deliver an anti-Catholic oration in Latin every November 5th in St Mary le Tower, a practice sensibly stopped by Mr King. During the eighteenth century, holidays were altered from a month during Christmas and August to 2 or 3 weeks at Christmas, Easter and Whitsun. As an endowed grammar school, only the classics and logic could legally be taught, although by about 1700 arithmetic, a branch of logic, had slipped in.

The purchasing power of the Headmaster's salary, fixed at a generous £24 a year by Wolsey and confirmed later by the Crown, had fallen 75 per cent by 1760. To top it up, the Town Council had spasmodically added and then subtracted and then sometimes added again small sums gleaned, often illegally, from various charities under its control, including Tooley's and Smart's as well as Felaw's own. Mr King's salary, a balance of the conflicting opinions in the town when he arrived, was £43.

The purpose of Felaw's charity, it may be remembered, had been to give a free education to a dozen or so poor boys. Nothing could be done about its income (£11 in 1718) once the little racket had been sorted out whereby a couple of the Corporation's creditors were allowed to occupy the charity's property at a peppercorn rent, but the number of boys it was supposed to support was capable of infinite variation. Sometimes it was 10, sometimes 20, sometimes 30 or 50. As the size of the school was limited, and the Headmaster could charge the market rate for teaching everyone else, this made a big difference to his income.

The trouble was that the poor scholars of the grammar school were not usually from the poorest families. Christ's Hospital and other charity schools now catered for them and got them apprenticeships. Many people understandably felt, therefore, that whatever the letter of Felaw's will, the spirit of his charity demanded that its money should go to Christ's Hospital, and from time to time this view prevailed. Moreover, if you were going to go back to medieval laws and usages, you could argue that the 'royal' salary of £24 was simply a bonus

The Rev. John King.

because in Felaw's day the Headmaster's remuneration came entirely from fees.

Several earlier Headmasters were so incensed by the Corporation's playing fast and loose with their income that they took it to Court with varying success. Mr King did not need to. During the eighteenth century, the clergy were steadily climbing the social and economic ladder and, with the rules for boarding numbers consequently relaxed, he was by no means badly off. Besides his free house and his Headmaster's salary and his £52 a year as Town Preacher, he could charge at least £30 a head per year for board and tuition. If half that was spent on feeding them, or other expenses, he was left with a profit of about £1,000 from 70 boarders. In addition, there were his fees from day boys, although with his quota of 30 free scholars, there cannot have been room for too many of them. He was also Rector of Witnesham which should have produced an annual £500 or more. That adds up to £1,600 a year, £80,000 today.

The school roof[1] became dangerous and in 1843 the school moved to a small insanitary house next to the Headmaster's who by 1850 was concentrating the Corporate mind on his problem by cleverly holding his senior classes in the Town Hall itself. A six-acre site near the top of Henley Road was acquired and a design for a new school agreed, a red-brick pastiche of Christ Church, Oxford, incorporating a replica of Wolsey's Gate by St Peter's church as an entrance porch.

There were 153 boys, mostly boarders, when the building was ready in 1852, only about 30 more than in Mr King's heyday in spite of the town's quadrupled population. This paucity of local day-boys had been a weakness ever since the prudent Elizabethan limit on boarding numbers had been extended. (One Headmaster in the 1830's appears to have recognised as much when he advertised an £8 discount on his £50 annual fees – single beds and possibly other luxuries were now

Ipswich School, Henley Road.

1. It was probably dismantled and taken to Cholderton near Andover where a church was built to fit it.

provided for everybody – if the boys came from Ipswich or adjacent parishes.)

No one cultivated a stand-off attitude to the town more studiously than the refined Dr Holden who became Headmaster in 1858. He did so not for financial reasons but to realise his ambition to put Ipswich among the country's great public schools recently made so fashionable by Dr Arnold of Rugby. For this he needed clever boys, preferably well-connected, rather than louts, suckers and cakes (to use contemporary school slang) from the town. An indecisive man, one of the most distinguished scholars of his day, he was a brilliant teacher of the sixth form but, outside it, totally lacking in charisma. Morals in the school were described by an old boy as 'unwholesome', and Dr Holden's long tenure of office (25 years) may well have been due to the skill of his second master, the Rev Mr 'Guts' Sanderson whose dedication, deceptively lumbering manner and puerile sense of humour made him universally popular.

Numbers at first grew annually. Ipswich had never been a very academic school, typically providing one Cambridge entrant a year. William Smart of Town Library fame and his wife's second husband, Ralph Scrivener, had endowed several small awards to help poor students through university (later merged into one Cambridge Exhibition), and Richard Martin another. Often candidates or standards were inadequate to take them up so, tontine-like, the cash accumulated for the next young man. Under Dr Holden, university scholarships, over and above any normal entrants, averaged nearly three a year, although by the 1870's school numbers were falling off - back to only 57 when, soon after Mr Sanderson's retirement, he resigned.

In 1881, the Endowed School Act transferred ultimate control of Ipswich School and Christ's Hospital from the Corporation to a tough governing body of 14, 11 locals and one each from the universities of Oxford, Cambridge and London. They engineered Dr Holden's resignation and in 1894 probably caused the suicide of Mr Browne, his successor.

Mr Browne, a hot-tempered Irishman, brought 43 boys with him from his previous school – perhaps the reason he was chosen – and his first term was consequently a tricky one. Thereafter he restored relations with the town and smartened up the boys' discipline and appearance. Local people were invited to concerts again, speechday – abolished by Dr Holden – brought back, and school outings organised into town for the theatre: 'I should have stated', Mr Browne added at the bottom of a notice announcing one such visit, 'that seats are

Dr. Holden at a cricket match.

offered in the *dress* circle'. He developed the maths and science side, building on Dr Holden's achievements, and started a Cadet Corps; that was soon disbanded after some trenchant comments by the inspecting officer on the standard of marching. By the time he was dismissed in 1894 over some policy disagreement, school numbers had reached 200.

Each in his own way, the next three Headmasters all seem slightly unsatisfactory. Mr Raynor tendered his resignation when he got into debt, and Mr Watson's was requested after a series of rows with the governors. Mr Sherwood survived to retirement at 60 but, a mild, earnest man with an overpowering wife, he, like Dr Holden, lacked charisma. Perhaps it was at his wife's suggestion that he put the boys into a pretentiously formal uniform of black coat, stiff collar and pinstriped trousers. In 1925 he purchased the Valley Road playing fields, his two predecessors having roused great enthusiasm for sport: Mr Raynor had returned full of athletic ideas from his earlier teaching and preaching in Australia, and Mr Watson, the first lay Headmaster for 200 years ('if anything, I suppose I am a Christian') was an Oxford cricket blue.

Not until 1920 did numbers exceed those achieved by poor Mr Browne. When the school became grant-aided in 1906, 10 per cent of its places were available free, but few applied to sit the required examination. The competition from other schools was hotting up.

In the old days, competition in the 'grammar' subjects of Latin, Greek and Logic had been kept at arm's length by the Bishop's licence. One man in 1667 had tried to set up as a grammar teacher in the town but was told a licence to do so would not be forthcoming. For most people the purpose of education was to learn to read the Bible; writing and grammar were pointless extras. Ipswich School took on its first writing-master in 1663, presumably after its entrance standard had been lowered to admit boys who couldn't.

During the 1680's Balthazar Gardemau, a writing-master and curate of St Mary Elms, taught immigrant Huguenots English in the later schoolroom next to the Town Library. He left his mark on the Library itself by inscribing his initials on about half its 600 volumes, and soon obtained preferment as parson at Coddenham, in due course moving in with his patron's widow to become squire of Shrublands.

Apart from Christ's Hospital, there were three other charity schools in Ipswich at the beginning of the eighteenth century, all modestly endowed: the Red Sleeve School for boys at its Master's house in Silent Street, and the boys' Grey Coat School with its sister foundation the girls' Blue Coat School nearby. (Confusingly, Christ's Hospital pupils were known as the Blue Coat boys.) In 1818 the three had a total of 156 children between them. As at Christ's Hospital, they were prepared for apprenticeship, being taught practical skills in the morning, and reading – and sometimes writing – in the afternoon. Some of the boys were apprenticed back to their fathers, so they, at least, came from reasonably prosperous homes. Subscribers supplemented the schools' endowment income, and £1 a year bought the right to nominate one pupil.

The nonconformist schools had subscribers only. The boys' Green Sleeve School was established in 1736 by the chapel in Tacket Street, and the girls' Green Gown in 1815, both very small. Most nonconformist children, if they went anywhere, were going by then to what were later known as the two 'British' schools (supported by the non-denominational British and Foreign School Society) the girls originally in St Matthew's Old Rectory and the boys in Crown Street; and both later in Turret Lane.

In 1818 there were 16 'public' or charity schools in Ipswich with

845 pupils. By 1870 there were nearly 4,000 in over 30 schools. There were also 10 private schools with 550 pupils in 1818, and around 60 with 2,000 in 1870 – 800 of them at 'superior' day or boarding schools and 1,200 at dame schools, most of which, according to the inspector, were bad and dirty. Thus overall, the proportion of the town's school-age population getting some kind of education had risen in the half-century between the two years from 45 to 60 per cent.

The growth in the public sector reflected the development of the parochial schools, by far the best being St Matthew's and St Peter's. The former had been set up in the Old Rectory after it was vacated by the girls' British School in 1848. It was enlarged to hold 500 or more – too big in the inspector's opinion who also mentions the schoolroom's painful echo. Hours were from 9am to 2pm for 5 days a week with no midday break since there was no playground. Fees were a penny a week, subsequently raised to 9 pence for the better-off who were increasingly attracted by its reputation. The layout of the boys' department was taken as a model by the later Board schools.

The boys of St Nicholas's paid 4 pence a week (parish resources didn't stretch to girls) which was topped up by subscriptions and the income from a small endowment. St Clement's and St Helen's School was mainly financed by the Rector of the two parishes who also built Holy Trinity church down the road and started its school. Both were rough schools in a rough area, the poorest and fastest growing in town.

The Ragged School was the only one to charge no fees at all. It was set up in 1849 in a couple of rooms in St Clement's on Quaker initiative to teach the rudiments to the very poorest boys and girls. Its first pupils were rounded up off the streets. As they had to earn a living during the day, classes were held on Sunday and weekday evenings – Tuesdays only at first. A schoolroom to hold 300 was purpose-built for them in 1858 in Waterworks Street. By then the curriculum included wood-chopping, cobbling and sewing at morning and afternoon classes. One boy was chosen to start up in town as a shoeblack but gave up after his 641st customer. Others were found jobs as uniformed porters in the Provisions Market. A night shelter was tried for a few years for the really destitute.

Ipswich was already regarded as one of the most educationally advanced towns in the country for the working classes when its School Board was formed in 1871 under the provisions of the great Education Act. Its purpose was to give schooling to everybody to the age of 13 in return for means-tested fees of up to 9 pence a week, which was roughly the cost per head of running a school. Using government loans and ratepayers' money, a total of 11 Board schools were built over the following years. The dame schools, and the Ragged School itself, were put out of business. Ragged School subscriptions fell from £363 to £17 in the year after the Board's establishment which at once took over its building as an infants' school. (The managers got it back nicely whitewashed 4 years later, and evening and Sunday classes continued there into the twentieth century.)

In spite of strong protestations from the Church, School Boards were non-denominational, and the Ipswich Board enjoyed a healthy tension between churchmen and nonconformists. Most members of the council were not specially interested in education – the Education Committee met just once a year to have dinner – so that, from the beginning, the Board was dominated by prominent outsiders who were. The exhortation of its Quaker chairman, Robert Ransome, that they were there not to produce little Dissenters or little Churchmen but good English Christian children fell largely on deaf ears, but on the whole, thanks to Ransome's tough leadership, it was an effective Board.

A few years later two working men joined it, Curtis George (but he was Tory and Church of England) and George Hines, a railway fireman and a leading light of the Co-op movement, who was openly scornful of its sectarian rivalries and demanded they should concentrate on helping the poor. He suggested, for example, that schools should issue children with shoes as well as books. This was turned down flat: the sixpenny school rate was already about half what was being spent on poor relief, and people were getting restive.

Somehow in 1880 Father Bennin got himself elected to the Board. Catholics, and especially Catholic priests, were not popular in nonconformist Ipswich, and he was accused among other things of being a 'great champion of Bible readings', a remarkably ignorant criticism to level against any Catholic. In fact his main concern was the development of school cookery classes – making pies and tarts, they said, with ratepayers' money. The Presbytery of one of his predecessors at St Pancras Church, which the Catholics had built twenty years previously in Orwell Place, had been besieged by a mob for 36 hours until the Police got round to relieving it. In 1871 a Catholic boys' school was put up nearby.

Nearly eighty years before that, Abbé Louis-Pierre Simon, a 25 year old refugee from the French Revolution, had arrived penniless in Upper Brook Street to teach French at Mr Carter's Boarding Academy. He continued to do so for 22 years when after Waterloo he was able to reclaim and sell his property in France. With the proceeds he bought a house and five acres on the 'healthy tableland' near the top of the Woodbridge Road. After various local objections and official obstruction, he built a chapel to St Anthony of Padua in the grounds, and opened a small school in the house. There were less than 60 Catholics in the town itself but his flock was augmented to 150 from the garrison and the surrounding countryside.

Father Simon left his property to the Catholic Church, and in 1860 the Sisters of Jesus and Mary set up a convent school for girls and infants in his five acres. Much enlarged, it is still there, a fitting memorial to a holy and dedicated man. What remained of his cash went towards the erection of St Pancras.

In 1878, the Girls' Public Day School Trust took over the Art School in the former Assembly Rooms in Northgate Street as a High School, the first in Ipswich offering girls a secondary education genuinely comparable to that of the boys' grammar school. It steadily expanded into adjacent houses, moved in 1907 to Westerfield Road, and in 1992 to Woolverstone Hall, the former home of the 'Cockney Eton', an ILEA experiment which had just been closed after bullying, vandalism and drug-taking had become endemic.

When the Endowed School governors were given control of the grammar school and Christ's Hospital in 1881, they also took over the town's various educational charities which they amalgamated and divided into 12 parts: 3 parts for a new girls' secondary school, 4 for a new boys' secondary school and 5 for the grammar school. Christ's Hospital after 300 years was closed down. The girls got its junior school in the southern half of the Blackfriars complex, and the boys its larger house in the Wherstead Road, on the old site of St Leonards leper hospital, but soon both were moved to more modern accommodation.

Fees were £6 a year and demand proved somewhat price-sensitive. After 10 years they had 200 boys and 100 girls on their books, figures which the School board's own Higher Grade School, opened in 1892 with fees of 6 pence a week, soon trebled.

About the same time, ignoring objections from the Working Men's College which didn't want subsidised competition, the Board started evening classes offering not only further elementary education for teenagers who had missed out at school but also subjects like playing the violin, typewriting and cookery.

Seven years later, the secondary and higher grade schools were merged as the boys' and girls' Municipal Secondary Schools in a building, gaunt even by the Board's unexacting standards, at Tower Ramparts. The girls were relocated in Bolton Lane in 1906 in spite of fears that that address might sound too much like a smelly back street if you didn't know it. By 1931 both establishments had been more happily renamed the Northgate Schools, and their pupils were re-united in Sidegate Lane where they still remain.

CHAPTER SEVENTEEN

From Cobbolds to cobbles

'NOT EXACTLY a benefactor ... his labours belong to the category of enlightened self-interest', wrote a Whig opponent of John Chevallier Cobbold after his election as an MP for Ipswich in 1847. That was at the height of his popularity, the year after the railway's arrival. Thirteen years later, on his father's death, relieved of all responsibility by the railway's insolvency and its imminent absorption into the Great Eastern, he took over the management of the brewery.

For the best part of a century, the family had followed a policy, familiar to players of Monopoly, of buying up promising little sites all over town so that, by now, managing property – an activity for which Cobbold with his solicitor's training was well suited – was becoming as important to the firm as brewing beer. Moreover, unlike other commodities, it was increasing in value. Some of it of course was used for taverns and ale-houses. At a property in Greyfriars Road one of the Cobbolds had discovered the foundation stone of Wolsey's St Mary's School, and rather meanly presented it to his old alumni at Christ Church, Oxford, instead of to Ipswich grammar school, its rightful owner.

As the population increased, streets were widened, houses developed or demolished, and improvements proposed. Cobbold was in the thick of it, a key landlord, sometimes agreeing, sometimes obstructing. When his eldest son, John Patteson, died in 1875, he pulled down some of his houses in Dog's Head Street and had it widened in his memory, a strange gesture. Felix Cobbold, in order to help his ageing father, and perhaps to succeed him, joined the firm and the family bank on his brother's death. In the event, in 1882, a grandson took over, John Patteson's eldest boy, John Dupuis, aged 22.

Felix remains the best remembered of the Cobbold clan in Ipswich because of his generous gift to the town of Christchurch Mansion. In 1735 the Christchurch estate had been sold by the grandson of the

The house at Hollywell's, west side (only the conservatory and stable tower remain).

Lord Hereford who was Charles II's dinner host, to a Huguenot merchant called Claude Fonnereau. The Fonnereaus paved the hall's old stone floor with chequered marble, opened up the front courtyard by removing the one-storey screen which joined the ends of the two wings, and modernised the interior. They kept the Park open to the public.

Six generations later, after the death of Thomas Fonnereau in 1891, the estate was put up for sale at £50,000. The Victorian Fonnereaus didn't think much of Ipswich (a dull town, it seemed to them, whose high rates were emptying the better houses) and they had already sold off substantial fringes of their land for housing development. To save the remainder from a similar fate, the Council was tempted to make an offer. As they couldn't agree, a referendum of ratepayers was held, and the proposal rejected.

Developments went ahead in Park Road and Bolton Lane, and plans drawn up to replace the Mansion itself with a crescent of superior houses. An open space round the crescent would obviously set it off much better than the rows of humbler dwellings which would certainly have followed in due course, and the Council was again offered what was left of the park for £16,250. They agonised for months until Felix Cobbold, having acquired the Mansion at the last minute, proposed to present it to the town on condition the park was bought to go with it. Thomas Fonnereau's mother was Felix's Aunt Kate, only recently deceased, and he was naturally concerned her beautiful home should escape the wreckers; but cynics, rightly or wrongly, have detected an ulterior motive.

Always a bachelor, his life does seem a curiously wasted one. After a brilliant career at Cambridge, he read for the Bar but never practiced. He became a Fellow of King's but never published a work of scholarship. In his 40's he entered Parliament as MP for Stowmarket but never made his mark there, giving up after a few months because of Conservative opposition to Irish Home Rule. It may be that like his brother John Patteson (a poor public speaker but an Ipswich MP for a year before his death) he was too meticulous for the crudities of Westminster. In 1896, the year after his gift of Christchurch Mansion, Felix who, perhaps because of the name, had chosen to live in Felixstowe, successfully put himself forward for the job of Mayor of Ipswich, a unique distinction for somebody neither resident nor on the Town Council; and later, at the age of 65, he briefly became one of the town's MP's, this time as a Liberal. On his death he left £20,000 to Christchurch Museum to provide a substantial endowment of £600 a year for the purchase of works of art. Inflation-adjusted, £600 is the equivalent of over £30,000 today. The capital, however, was cautiously invested, and its income, currently around £2,000, has failed to keep pace.

While Christchurch Mansion had been owned by just two families before it was given to the Corporation, The Chantry off the Hadleigh Road, 150 years younger, had been owned by nine. It originally comprised land left by Edmund Daundy, Wolsey's uncle or cousin, to provide a modest income for his chantry in St Lawrence's church. Its first recorded house was put up in 1688 by Mr Justice Ventris, the man chiefly responsible for the Shire Hall being built to attract the Assizes from Bury.

By 1772, the property was in the hands of Metcalfe Russell, a young hypochondriac, who claimed to have been cured of something by Mrs Coward's Ipswich Spa Waters in St Margaret's, its only known success.

Eighty years and two owners later it was bought by 'Applepip' Kelly QC, now Sir Fitzroy, one of the two Tory MPs who had been locked up in Newgate after the bribery scandal of 1835. He built the estate's Golden Gates on the Hadleigh Road – on show at the Great Exhi-

Felix Cobbold.

bition – and converted the house's Georgian elevations into the Italian style, a flamboyant version of Ipswich station. Fortunately he was less drastic with its fine interior.

In 1927 The Chantry and its land were purchased by Arthur Churchman (later Lord Woodbridge) the 'A. C.' of W. A. and A. C. Churchman, and presented to the town. A few years later he bought Holywell's Park from the Cobbolds and presented that also to Ipswich. His firm was old but his money new. Since 1790 the Churchmans had sold their own snuff and tobacco from a well-placed shop equidistant from Cornhill and the Barracks beside the site of the old Westgate, absurdly renamed Hyde Park Corner. They hit the big time after the naughty nineties had launched the cigarette on an innocent world.

Just as Ipswich had rewarded Felix Cobbold by electing him Mayor,

Sir Fitzroy Kelly, Q.C.

so Churchman's generosity was acknowledged by appointing him to the ancient sinecure of High Steward. Like an elective constitutional monarchy, it was conferred for life on a prominent figure enjoying some connection with Ipswich, however tenuous. Sir Francis Walsingham, Queen Elizabeth's Secretary of State, and her boy friend, the Earl of Essex, both accepted the honour; Robert Cecil, Walsingham's successor, refused it. Nelson was chosen on the strength of his purchase of Roundwood, and Kitchener because on his mother's side he was a Chevallier. Wellington, a Tory, foolishly allowed his name to go forward in an undignified contest in 1821 and lost. John Chevallier Cobbold became High Steward after he retired from Parliament.

The Nelsons bought the 55-acre Roundwood estate in 1797, and sold it in 1800 after their separation. It was just beyond the barracks in the Woodbridge Road, then a tree-lined boulevard, at its junction with Rushmere Road. Nelson never slept in the house, but his wife and father spent some time there. Lady Nelson was feted in the Assembly Room at the celebration of her husband's victory on the Nile, but she had little in common with the 'Tabby Cats' who normally frequented it and the adjacent coffee houses.

Nelson paid £2,000 for Roundwood and sold it for £3,300, the added value being primarily a monetary reflection of his fame. It was bought for £7,860 in 1899 by a building society. The house with some of the land was sold back to the sitting tenant for £5,000, converted in the twentieth century into seedy flats, and ultimately demolished by the Church to make way for St John's Primary School in 1961.

The purpose of the building society movement was to enable more people to acquire land with a value of at least £10 and so extend the franchise. The first in Ipswich was the Freehold Land Society (now the Ipswich Building Society) which was founded in 1849. Within a decade the Second Reform Act had rendered its political point obsolete, but it continued with undiminished vigour. Land, whose price was slowly rising, was more attractive now than votes priced at zero.

The Society paid a market rate for loans and deposits, between 6½ per cent and 8 per cent, and charged 5 per cent. This was viable because of the difference between the wholesale and retail cost of land where substantial blocks could be purchased, and then sold off piecemeal at a profit. It was essentially a highly-geared dealing operation, and rightly considered risky by investors. Only the overt backing of

Roundwood.

Alexanders Bank enabled the Society to ride the national property crisis of 1892 without a fall and to obtain money as cheaply as it did.

Its first purchase was 100 acres of Cauldwell Hall farmland to the east of St Helen's. With no shortage of applicants it was divided into 282 plots of about one-third of an acre. The price was fixed at £21.50 each, repayable at a minimum rate of one shilling and sixpence a week, so that the borrower would be free from debt within about six years. The Society's expenses, including legal and other fees plus £480 for roadworks, was £20 a plot. Sewerage and water were the responsibility of the new freeholders.

As demand grew, the Society was emboldened to undertake some development itself. The price of 28 'pretty' 6-roomed cottages on 80 foot plots which were erected and balloted for in Palmerston and Lancaster Roads, went at once to a modest premium on their £145 asking figure; 12 years later they were changing hands at £180. The ballot in 1894 attracted 4,190 applicants for 89 properties.

Most borrowers could afford a plot only: they might grow vegetables on it or, if they wanted a house built, do it themselves. A daily stream of hopefuls could now be seen heading off along Spring Road with picks and shovels. Many used stones dug out of their land rather than expensive bricks – 'digging their graves', said a sour observer. The forty-niners and the gold rush were in the news and although Ipswich's new frontier was east instead of west, the district became known as California.

By 1890 there were few areas in and around Ipswich where the Society had not dealt. Woodruffe Daniel, its solicitor since the very beginning, died in that year. It was a prestigious and well-paid job (£400 a year and part time) and it seemed every solicitor in town was after it. Under the Society's antiquated rules, only shareholders (borrowers as well as depositors) could decide the matter.

A meeting was held in the Corn Exchange, standing room only, which 1,600 people attended. All had one vote, including children down to a baby depositor of 6 months. The transport for many had been laid on by the candidates, now whittled down to three: Jewesson, Ridley, Ward. On a show of hands, Jewesson got 8 votes. Laughter all round, including the unhappy Jewesson. Everybody seemed to vote for the other two – large and small hands, wrote a reporter, gloved, delicate and horny – so 40 minutes were spent counting them all out through separate exits into the street. They trooped back to hear that Ridley, a sporty 32-year-old, had won. Then the rules were changed.

At the turn of the century, exactly 50 years after the first sod had been turned on the Cauldwell Hall estate, the work of dealing with its sewage was nearing completion. California had seen severe outbreaks of diphtheria and diarrhoea in 1895, so the matter was considered urgent, which is why it had only taken 5 years so far.

The town centre itself had long possessed a number of shallow and quite inadequate sewers; they discharged into the river near the Common Quay via an outlet which had to be moved to below the gasworks when the Wet Dock was built. Peter Bruff, the railway engineer, designed a more up to date sewage system in 1857, and with modifications this went ahead 22 years later. Bruff's outlet and treatment plant were a mile downstream at Hog Highland, previously a popular picnic spot. Thereafter, until steps were taken in 1932 (after the Sanitary Authority's diagnosis of the pollution as decaying seaweed was proved nonsense) it was the famed source of Orwell Odours.

Although the connection between disease and drains was well accepted, the trouble was that sewers meant not only higher rates but actual loss of income, for sewage had a value. It was stored beside the house until there was enough for a farmer to collect. Before the fertilisers of Joseph Fison and his kind, the cost of buying-in 5 cwt of either guano or farm manure – enough for an acre – was £1. One adult was reckoned to produce as much per annum, a useful addition to the family budget, especially now that the vote was worthless. Ipswich in fact was an important entrepot for sewage which arrived from London by the boatland for distribution round Suffolk.

The Wet Dock's construction also caused the closure of the town's three bathing establishments: John Barnard's in St Clement's, a second only a few years old by St Mary Quay, boasting hot salt water plus vapour and shower baths, and a third in Stoke off the Wherstead Road. This was owned by a man called Staton who in 1820 advertised his charges: a shilling for ladies and gentlemen and half price for children. Subscription for a single person was 15 shillings a year (rather cheaper than Barnard's) and for husband and wife or for two ladies, 21 shillings. Group membership for boarding schools was 42 shillings. All three pools were replaced by another in Stoke, owned and run by the Corporation, 100 yards long, at the bottom of the New Cut and filled by tidal water. For a century it was the town's chief bathing place, and despite the Orwell Odours, the focus every summer of the Ipswich Regatta. In 1894 another pool was constructed upstream by the Gipping near Handford Bridge. As it had no bottom, the water quickly seeped out. A concrete floor was added but it was always slimy and never watertight. Mixed bathing started in 1917. The river became polluted and it was closed in 1935.

The town's principal water supply had always been the Corporation springs in the area of Cauldwell Hall. By 1848 nearly 1,500 homes were taking this water from a couple of mains in Carr Street. As many others had water piped to them from a number of privately-owned reservoirs, chiefly the Cobbolds' at Holywell, the Alexanders' (the Quaker bankers) in St Matthew's, and the Waterworks Company's in St Clement's. The town's 4,000 other houses relied on public pumps or their own wells, most of which were contaminated.

The inhabitants of Ipswich, having few facilities for washing, were not extravagant with their water. In 1862, to the inspector's horror, they were using only 14 gallons a day per head. New York and ancient Rome, he said, used 300, and even London and Glasgow were consuming 50. Could Ipswich ever compete? And if it did, would supplies by sufficient? The Gipping was suggested as an additional source, but its water was much harder – 50 per cent harder than London's – and it was estimated this would cost housewives an extra £1,200 a year in soap alone.

Pressure to do something came in particular from the new homes on the higher ground of the Fonnereaus' northern suburb whither the rich were migrating. There was no need of lobbying: many members of the Council had moved there themselves. The Waterworks Company built a reservoir off Park Road but it was soon too small. The Company was bought by the Corporation in 1892 and the Council at once embarked on a comprehensive scheme. This included hydrants at strategic points, so that someone calculated that the inevitable rise in rates would rapidly be recouped from lower fire insurance premiums. By the time California got its sewers, virtually every one of the town's houses, now totalling 14,000, had running water. Even so, they were only using 20 gallons a day per head.

Queen Elizabeth's pointed comments on the state of Ipswich streets had had only a temporary effect. Since her sister's reign, the parishes had been responsible for maintaining them through a system of compulsory labour of 6 days a year from all able-bodied male householders (and later through a Highways Rate) until in 1793 the Corporation obtained powers to raise money for the repair and upkeep of the main thoroughfares. By 1796 a visitor discovered 'the whole town was paved ... excepting St Clement's which was doing', a landmark in its history.

Sometimes cobbles and setts were used, and sometimes 6oz granite chips as recommended by the meticulous MacAdam (small boys were set to work with scales and hammers) but neither method proved satisfactory. Cracks and potholes soon filled with rotting rubbish, and streets had to be sluiced with fresh or salt water, latterly enriched by carbolic when in hot weather the stench became too bad. Those who had cobbles in their street wanted it MacAdamised or vice-versa, and the Council, not knowing the answer, usually obliged. Even if the Council had known, no road could have coped for long with the ceaseless building activity of the nineteenth century: the replacement of the carved timber frames of Tooley's age with the depressing grey bricks of Ransome's: the transformation of Tudor gutters into the sanitation of the late Victorians: the ruthless remodelling of almost every church.

Many pavements were laid with flagstones on which artists were able to earn a few pennies until this harmless occupation was forbidden because it was being exploited as an advertising medium. In the 1870's there were some messy experiments with tar paving, and it was 10 years before the advantages of steam-rolling were appreciated.

Waterloo House, 1883.

The main streets started to be paved with wood blocks when horse-trams were introduced in the early 1880's. They ran from the station to Cornhill and from the Barracks in St Matthew's to Major's Corner, extending west and east from Bramford Lane to Derby Road where the new Felixstowe railway had a station.

The tram opened up Carr Street which alone of the town's central arteries had escaped widening, having been by-passed in the 1820's by the construction of Great Colman Street as a more direct link between Tavern Street and the Woodbridge Road. As Alexander Nicolson realised when he was Mayor in 1887, Carr Street was ripe for development. His project was an ambitious but undercapitalised private one, involving both sides of almost the entire street, and he said – improbably – that it nearly ruined him. In fact his own money at risk seems to have been no more than the £3,500 subsidy he extracted from the Council. There was a story that he had been cajoled into the whole thing: one can take that too with a pinch of salt. But at least for its money the Council got the street widened by 10 feet although it had to pay for its resurfacing afterwards.

Nicolson for 50 years had been junior partner in Footman, Pretty and Nicolson of Waterloo House in Westgate Street, by now the town's largest and grandest draper's shop. It had been founded in 1815 by an uncle of the John Footman who was briefly manager of the Eastern Union. John died in 1854 worth £32,000 or nearly £2m. today. His two sons had joined the firm but discovered drapery bored them. Henry, having with difficulty married one of the Quaker Ransomes, left to become a Parson, and Fred whose entanglements with girls and horses were thought to be upsetting customers, was given a golden handshake to get out. Just before Nicolson's death in 1892, the business, along with its corset factory at the back on Tower Ramparts (joined to the shop by a footbridge over the road) was acquired by the Prettys. They had built up what was virtually a corset monopoly in the town. The shop was bought by Debenhams in 1927, and took its parent's name in 1972.

Opposite, on the corner of Cornhill and Westgate Street, was another draper, J H Grimwade. The Bell tavern had for many years been on the corner itself, with Grimwades next door, until in 1873 a temperance consortium bought it up and granted a lease to a tailor called Poole, presumably because he was teetotal and Grimwade was not. It cost Grimwade the substantial sum of £700 to buy him out. And by 1904 the shop, which achieved the distinction of being the first in Ipswich to stock Dr Jaeger's Sanitary Woollen Goods, had been extended to its present appearance.

On the town's main axis (Westgate Street, Cornhill and Tavern Street) drapers and tailors easily predominated – 26 in 1881, or one shop in every five. Grocers were a poor second with ten, and shoemakers third with eight. Chemists and jewellers (including Croydons) numbered six each. There were five wine merchants plus as many taverns.

In the centre of Cornhill was a cab rank which for a brief two years enjoyed the use of an imposing drivers' shelter beside it. But it was found cabbies were missing fares by using it, and in 1895 it was removed in one piece to Christchurch Park, inside the Bolton Lane entrance where it still remains. A Memorial to the dead of the Boer War was later erected on Cornhill in its place. That too soon ended up in Christchurch Park.

Two other large businesses near the centre of town, both with tall belching chimneys, were Cowells, since 1818 printers in Buttermarket (supposedly on the site of Reginald Oliver's pre-Reformation pub-

Edward Grimwade.

lishing house) and, until it was burnt down in 1848, the Anglesey Paper Mills off what is now Grimwade Street.

This was named after Edward Grimwade, not one of the drapers but a related worthy who was thrice Mayor. After his death, his home and wholesale chemist's warehouse in Fore Street, near or over the mediaeval public latrines, became the heated Corporation Baths.

Felix Cobbold, having presented the land and helped with the Bath's building costs, made a speech at the opening ceremony in 1894 which must have caused some embarrassment: 'I have been told', he said, 'that in some aristocratic towns (I am glad Ipswich is not one of them) there are different classes, the first class ladies one day, the first class gentlemen another, and then at the end of the week, when the water is dirty, the poor are admitted.' In fact these were exactly the arrangements the Council had decided upon; nor is there any record they were changed when Cobbold became Mayor 18 months later.

The interior of the Town Hall had altered little in six centuries, and the neat Palladian facade it acquired in 1818 merely concealed its problems. It was complained the premises were too small, the roof was unsafe (once it had actually collapsed during a Council Meeting) and the basement, occupied by the Police, was too damp – as no doubt it had been since St Mildred's was deconsecrated to become the Town Hall, but standards, as well as the level of Cornhill, had risen.

In 1854 the Council advertised a competition with a first prize of £105 for the design of a new building, twice the size of the old one after demolition of the shop and tavern adjoining its east side; 28 entries were received but none was suitable. 'Do I understand', asked Edward Grimwade at the next Council Meeting, 'that we are bound to give someone the prize even if the plans do not deserve it?' The Mayor replied that the best plan was after all the best, and because of the way the advertisement was drafted, entitled to the prize. There was an outcry about the waste of ratepayers' money which was now producing around £40,000 a year for the Council to spend.

Slowly, however, over a period of 10 years, one of runners-up, in the style of a Venetian palazzo, emerged as the favourite. The architect made some practical and aesthetic modifications which kept the estimate within the Council's budget of £10,000, although, as Grimwade remarked (as Councillors are wont to remark) the price – '£7,000, £8,000 or £10,000' – was comparatively immaterial. The lowest tender in fact turned out to be for £11,749. ('I have so many

John Patteson Cobbold.

rates and taxes to pay these days', commented Grimwade a little later, 'that I confess I have almost become radical'. Cry of 'Nonsense'.) The building one sees today does less than justice to the original: many important decorative features have fallen off over the years and not been replaced.

John Patteson Cobbold was Mayor in 1868 and the organisation of the celebrations for the opening week displayed his meticulous talents to the full: a Conversatzione on Monday, a Ball on Tuesday, bell-ringing from St Mary le Tower throughout Wednesday, a men-only Banquet on Thursday and a children's party on Friday. Wednesday was also the day of the first Council Meeting in its new Chamber and the presentation to the Mayor of fresh robes. 'I need not for one moment assert', his reply began, 'that the wearing of a new gown will neither add to the dignity of the position which I occupy nor in any way make me or others who succeed me more desirous of doing that simple thing, our duty, in our high position'. After a Ball on the previous night, one cannot take too much of that sort of thing.

They had another matter to discuss that day: what to do about the clock? In the past, the Town Hall clock had used the Ipswich meridian, five minutes ahead of Greenwich. Was it appropriate, with all the publicity they were receiving, that Ipswich time should remain different from the rest of the country? The railway of course kept Greenwich time, and someone suggested it was useful to have that little extra in hand if you were catching a train. 'We keep time by the sun, and surely that is enough?' And so, until 1881, it was.

Other buildings also, which scarcely a generation earlier had been erected or renovated with such high enthusiasm, had become outdated or derelict. The Regency Corn Exchange, having been expensively modernised in 1850, was replaced in 1881 by today's larger and duller version behind the Town Hall. Its position on Cornhill was taken by a new Post Office; (by 1993 that too had evidently outlived its usefulness). The Provisions Market, after its refurbishment in 1867, was reduced to advertising its declining merits with the enigmatic initials QCE above its main gate (Quality, Civility and Excellence?) and in 1888 its stalls were removed to the new Corn Exchange. Likewise in 1856 the Cattle Market was shifted due west to a larger and less inconvenient location on the other side of Princes Street, while part of its old site was planted with trees. The Mechanics', or Ipswich,

Corn Exchange, 1855.

Institute in Tavern and Tower Streets, set up in 1824 by a group which included poor George Bayley, the shipwright, was remodelled for its fiftieth anniversary. And the Museum of Museum Street (1847) a private Quaker initiative, soon became inadequate for patrons and exhibits alike. Its evening openings free of charge were especially popular with the poorer townspeople, much to the Curator's annoyance: a vile, disorderly mob, they were, smelly, noisy and scattering litter.

At 10.39 on a July morning of 1851 a minor panic gripped the town's dignitaries assembled at Halifax Junction: the Prince Consort's train was approaching, 5 minutes early, and there was no Mayor. But all was well, and with seconds to spare he was correctly positioned when the Prince stepped out. Rose petals covered the carpeted platform whose every cranny was stiff with laurel branches. There were flags and more laurel in the marquee where the Prince 'with all the blandness ... of a finished gentleman' listened to an address of welcome. Behind the scenes,, on the Queen's special instructions, a message was telegraphed to Buckingham Palace that he had arrived safely.

Then off by carriage with Mayor and Astronomer Royal to visit the seven sections of the British Association whose twenty-first Annual Meeting was being held in the town. He spent half an hour at each one, seated beside the presiding officer while the paper or discussion continued.

Next morning, having spent the night at Shrublands, he inspected the Museum and had lunch among the exhibits. Afterwards he laid the foundation stone of Ipswich School in the Henley Road. The Museum had impressed him greatly. The Queen remarked that for several days he talked of little else. Was he surprised a few months later to receive a request for money? The Museum was bankrupt, £500 in debt, and had to be taken over by the Corporation. He promised £100 towards clearing the debt, provided the townspeople raised the balance, which they did.

In a triumphal gesture, the Wet Dock's new entrance lock, the new Post Office, and the Corporation's spacious new Museum in the High Street were all opened on the same day, July 27th 1881. And just as the Queen's Golden Jubilee, six years later, symbolised the high point of Victorian expansion, that day of triple celebration did the same for Ipswich. The nineteenth century was ending early, as centuries often do.

CHAPTER EIGHTEEN

Labour

NOT ALL the one-up, one-down tenements in the 100 or more courts and alleys where the poor lived were insanitary, nor all their inhabitants destitute. There was many a dwelling whose walls were whitewashed, whose tiny non-opening windows sparkled, and whose floors and furniture were daily scrubbed; whose latrine, shared with several others, was somehow cared for. Dickens towards the end of his life visited Ipswich a number of times for sessions of his famous readings, and he went so far as to comment that 'to the casual observer' there was no sign in the town of abject poverty. He certainly would not have seen too much of it on a stroll between The Great White Horse and the Corn Exchange where he usually performed.

Abject or not, a working man was still earning little more in real terms than his Domesday forebears – up to 22 shillings for a 60-hour week in the case of bricklayers and carpenters in 1872. The Cock and Pye in Upper Brook Street was their union headquarters, and in that year they embarked on a month's successful strike for 4 shillings a week more pay and Saturday afternoons off. The workers at Ransomes, whose engineering staff had already secured the latter, raised £80 to help them out. Engineers, the town's elite, had been unionised since the 1840's: there were 84 members in 1851, 33 in 1855 and 200 by 1900. Dockers followed in 1890, and railway servants, postmen, painters and decorators, plumbers and tram workers soon after. During the first dozen years of the twentieth century, a number of them experimented with the strike weapon with varying success. Bricklayers' wages were nearly £2 for a 56½-hour week by 1909, while since 1872 prices had risen only marginally.

The tram workers by contrast were receiving only 14 shillings for a 70-hour week in 1896. The Tramways Company was said to be one of the worst employers in the business, partly because for most of its life it was insolvent and in receipt of a small subsidy from the Corporation to keep it going. In 1898 fares had to be reduced to compete with the

Horse-tram.

Penny Omnibus Company whose 18 horse-buses began to offer a cheaper and more flexible alternative to the 9 trams.

The tram company in which Alexander Nicolson and his associates had invested around £40,000, was compulsorily acquired by the Corporation in 1901 for £17,500. Both parties reckoned they had got a bargain. It was a couple of years before the Council realised otherwise, when trams, horses and the rest of the stock were sold off to make way for 10 miles of new track (more than double the old route), 26 new electric cars, and a new depot at the Corporation's generating plant in Constantine Road. Trams and Power Station were managed by the same committee, and in the early years the trams took half its electricity. In 1904 power generation made a profit of £9,000, four times as much in real terms as its vastly enlarged successor by Cliff Quay in 1970.

Against all the evidence, the trams too were expected to make a profit, but they never did. Once, the Council suspended a tram worker without pay for reporting two minutes late for duty, and the following Sunday before a crowd on Cornhill the union cleverly staged a tableau to re-enact the scene. Lack of profit produces meanness in the most well-intentioned employer, a lesson the twentieth century has been slow to learn.

Many of the new tracks were laid on streets paved with cobbles rather than wood blocks, and the rival horse-buses and other vehicles aimed to keep to them to get a smoother ride. The tracks wore out quickly as a result, which became a problem during the First World War when iron and steel were scarce. After the war, the horse-buses were replaced by Tilling's motor variety, both faster and cheaper, so that the Council took the opportunity to impose a minimum fare on their service within the town to limit competition.

It was recognised by now that the old trams were uneconomic. What about battery-operated ones, dispensing with unsightly overhead wires and their maintenance? Ransomes thought they could supply them, but fortunately failed to persuade the Council. What about trolleybuses, dispensing with costly rails? Ransomes again were enthusiastic, and quoted a keen price for the new conveyances. And so, in 1926, Ipswich became one of only two Corporations in the country to switch entirely to the trolleybus. (That was an awkward word, so the monosyllabic tram remained in use.) Trolleybuses were

The Hippodrome (after 1959, The Savoy Ballroom).

no more economic, and the vibration from their solid tyres not only produced a rough ride but did extensive damage to the ceilings of houses along their route.

No one in 1926 had foreseen the blackout, and at the beginning of the second war, once day-time services had ended, the whole wiring system, covering 25 miles by this time, had to be overhauled by torchlight, and gadgets fitted called carbon slipper collectors to stop the electric flashes as the trolley buses went by. Most of the original 30, now with pneumatic tyres, plus 10 double-deckers added in 1933, survived the war. Thirty-eight replacements were delivered between 1945 and 1948, only to be expensively exchanged from 1950 onwards for diesel motorbuses. But at least by then the town's electricity generation was no longer so dependent on their custom, and in any case had been nationalised.

The Co-operative Society's retail operations had started in 1869 from dark little premises in Carr Street. After the tram's arrival and as part of the street's improvement, a grand new shop was built and steadily extended eastwards. By 1920 the Society had 10 branches, and its store in Carr Street was probably the most extensive in town.

The Co-op's commercial thinking was less radical than its politics. It would have made more money and had a greater influence for better or worse on the town's development, had it moved decisively westwards nearer Cornhill. It had outgrown Carr Street which, despite its presence, remained a shopping backwater: the Lyceum, the offices of the East Anglian Daily Times, a rifle range, a motor engineer, a couple of bicycle shops, the gas showrooms, a florist or two, but little else. Shoppers still favoured Westgate and Tavern Streets where, with a few additions such as a YMCA gym and a stockbroker, the pattern had changed little in fifty years. Multiples had begun to appear – Marks & Spencer's bazaar and Sainsburys in Westgate Street, for example, and Boots in both Westgate Street and Tavern Street.

Although for nine months in 1924 Ipswich had been a Parliamentary Labour stronghold (electors since the war had one vote only, and the town one MP) the General Strike two years later received only a muted response. The Co-op continued deliveries to its member households, comprising over half the town's total, and 300 of the most needy were given a 5 shilling voucher. Employees of the Co-op Insurance Society, whose union only achieved recognition in 1929 after a strike both for that purpose and a minimum wage, also seem to have remained aloof. Foundry workers were already on short time – Ransomes had earlier laid off 1,500 – and they were not called out.

Nor were construction workers, on the grounds that many of them were building working-class homes; some of those that did strike lost their jobs. The Corporation's transport workers came out, and none of their union officials were reinstated afterwards. Power workers came out, but, as expected, they were immediately replaced by naval ratings. In all, little more than 4,000 out of the town's employed workforce, male and female, in the region of 25,000 took part.

Mr R F Jackson, the forgotten stonemason who in 1924 was Ipswich's first Labour MP, had also in 1911 become its first Labour Councillor, and the first to propose the construction of Council houses. A few years previously, the Council, as required by Parliament, had built 20 in Devonshire Road, St Clement's, to rehabilitate families displaced by the electric tramway, only to find that since they were of a cramped and mean design more common in Lancashire than Suffolk, the families had made their own arrangements. There had earlier been a surplus of 700 units round the town, but in 1911 there was a shortage. The typical 5 shilling rental had already risen by 6 pence a week, and in addition the Council was beginning to think it should do something about clearing the slums; a matter given some urgency by the recent diagnosis of an old enemy in the town, bubonic plague.

Jackson proposed the Corporation's 26 acres between the Hadleigh and London Roads should be developed. That should be enough for up to 300 houses and, as he hoped, put a stop to the rise in rents, especially if they were offered at 3 shillings a week 'which no private builder could meet'. They were eventually built in 1920, the first of the Council's 4,000 put up between the wars primarily as slum replacements. But, as with the tramway houses, the municipal monotony of their design persuaded many of the former slum-dwellers to look elsewhere.

In 1939, the Council had 220 houses on its hands and – until the bombs began to fall – no takers. Thereafter it evolved a formula which, as Jackson had realised, should guarantee a contented and plentiful tenantry – better accommodation and subsidised rents. Seven thousand more were constructed in the 20 years to 1965, giving the Council ownership of nearly one-third of the town's housing stock. Rents, which in 1920 were 15 shillings a week on Jackson's Hadleigh Road estate (the inflation-adjusted equivalent of the pre-war 5 shillings) started at just 16 shillings in 1965.

Bombs in neither war were of much help in slum clearance. Zeppelins made over a dozen attacks between 1915 and 1918 and

The Barracks: Officers' Mess. (They were closed down in 1929.)

seriously damaged the riverside bathing pool at Stoke. In the second war there were 1,165 alerts but only about 50 bombing raids in which 255 houses were destroyed, conveniently eliminating the Council's surplus.

The Germans' main effort against Ipswich during the Second World War, through both attempted sabotage and bombing raids, was directed at the Crane factories off the Nacton Road which were important munitions suppliers. Forty bombs landed on or round them in one raid in May 1941 and put them out of action for five days. Richard T. Crane was a Chicago manufacturer of plumbing products who opened his UK operations here in 1926. It was said he chose Ipswich because he had a little holiday home, similar in style and scale to Christchurch Mansion, overlooking the bay at Ipswich, Massachusetts.[1]

When the Wet Dock was first constructed, maltings of modest size and elegant two-storied warehouses overhanging an iron colonnade

1. There is also an Ipswich in South Dakota, another in Minneşota and a third in Jamaica. There is a New Ipswich in New Hampshire. The largest Ipswich outside Suffolk is near Brisbane in Queensland, Australia, with a population of over 50,000.

went up either side of the new Customs House which rightly remained the dominant building on the town-side waterfront. By 1939 it had been dwarfed by the vast and shabby constructions of the twentieth century, prominent flammable targets for the German bombers, but only some were hit, one literally by a crashing raider.

As trade expanded during the years before the First World War, the whole of the far side of the dock (the 'island site' of the Promenade and the tide-mill basin) was concreted over for more quays – needless vandalism as it turned out because in 1923 work was started on an entirely new complex at Cliff Quay, downstream from the dock entrance. Shell-Mex and Fisons bought land behind it for their industrial use, and in 1937 a Power Station was begun nearby with a dreary little Customs House beside it. By 1960 Cliff Quay and its extensions continued for nearly three-quarters of a mile down the river's east shore, while during the 1970's the West Bank Terminal was developed opposite. The medieval concept of the Port of Orwell had been realised, and was soon to become with the addition of the docks at Felixstowe, the largest in Europe. In the middle ages Ipswich and Harwich had wrangled over its control. Today Felixstowe, controlled by a Chinese owner, is by a large margin the major partner; and the Dock at Ipswich, a decaying mess, the town's powerhouse for 50 generations, is almost deserted.

The demise of the Wet Dock completed the town's transformation from a commercial to an industrial centre, from making money to earning it. The cloth cap had finally supplanted the 'beaver hat' of Chaucer's merchants. Labour was the master now.

At the beginning of the Second World War as over the previous century, more people were employed in engineering than in anything else, but countless other industries had come and gone, or in some cases expanded beyond recognition, since the early days of shipbuilding, beer and ploughshares.

Pretty's corset factory now covered 3 acres, and with 1,500 employees was said to be the world's largest producer of artificial silk underwear. Phillips and Piper had been making cheap suits since 1851, and Firmins sacks and tarpaulins since soon after its foundation as linen weavers with Huguenot labour in 1682.

Turners the tanners had operated from the Bramford Road since the eighteenth century. The Churchmans in 1897 had moved their cigarette making from the shop at Hyde Park Corner to a factory in Portman Road which between the wars was several times extended. During the 1920's William Brown rented a log pickling pool near the

Churchman's Shop, beside a canvas mock-up of the Westgate.

Stoke bathing place and expanded its timber interests into the grounds of Handford Lodge, the former charming home of the town's sewage consultant and the Eastern Union engineer, Peter Bruff.

British Oil and Cake Mills had been crushing linseed at the north-east corner of Stoke Bridge since about 1885 when its former premises at Handford Mill were burnt down. Across the road, at the bridge's north-west corner, the Stoke tide-mill which Fisons had acquired and converted to steam, was now a yeast factory of British Fermentation Products. And towering over the Wet Dock, between the linseed mill and the Customs House, rose the buildings of three of the largest non-engineering enterprises in town, Cranfield's flour mill, Burton Son and Sanders, the confectioners, and the maltings and silo of R and W Paul.

Robert and William Paul were still in their teens when they inherited their father's barge business in 1864 – all sailing barges. Grain was their main cargo but they carried anything available including scrap iron to Newcastle or dung from London. Gradually the small, old-style maltings with their distinctive cowls disappeared from

Cubbitt's Stoke Bridge, replaced 1925.

behind the warehouses at the dock, and in 1885 the Pauls built their first modern one on the quayside.

The firm prospered, especially during the first war when freight rates rose six-fold, double the increase in prices generally. The barges' shallow draught enabled them to cross minefields unharmed, and their small size to avoid the attention of enemy submarines. In the second war, four were towed across the Channel to take part in the evacuation of Dunkirk. The crew of one of them laboriously rowed the last leg of the journey inshore under cover of darkness (shipping their oars out of the phosphorescent sea whenever aircraft appeared) and took off 273 troops. The other three barges, laden with stores, had to be abandoned. Next day, soldiers emptied one and returned in it naked to Dover, their Commanding Officer preserving his dignity with a strip of carpet.

In 1896 Cobbold's Cliff Brewery, patched, extended and obsolescent after more than a century of use, was completely rebuilt. Eight years before, John Dupuis, the senior partner, still in his twenties, had committed a small oversight which was to have portentous repercussions: Cullingham's Brewery of Upper Brook Street came on the

Queen Victoria's statue in front of Christchurch Mansion (demolished in Second World War).

market and he allowed it to be snapped up by a couple of young men of about his own age, Stanhope and Douglas Tollemache. They developed the site, and achieved with Tolly ale in one generation almost as much as the Cobbolds had achieved in six. When Catchpole's Unicorn Brewery, the only other of significance in the town, was closed in 1923, the two firms shared its assets, deciding their division by the toss of a coin. And when they were merged in 1957, the name chosen for the new combine was Tollemache and Cobbold, and not the other way round.

Nowhere was Cobbold influence more impressive than in the matter of Ipswich Town Football Club. Formed in 1878 as an amateur club, the highlight of its year was a vicious match against Harwich 'too rough to be dangerous' in the words of one Ipswich spectator who had innocently bothered to count the goals. By 1936, standards were higher, but apparently not much, and many people who now had Saturday afternoons off, resented having to travel to Norwich or London to see serious football. The club, however, in spite of heavy pressure, refused to alter its amateur status, and a separate professional club, aggressively misnamed Ipswich United, was born. In mid-April the Town club held a special meeting in the Town Hall, instead of its usual venue at the Inkerman in Chevallier Street, to reaffirm its decision, and to make arrangements for sharing the Corporation's ground at Portman Road with the newcomer.

On April 24th an abrupt letter appeared out of the blue in the evening paper: 'Sir, on my return from Canada today I am delighted to hear that the question of a professional football side for Ipswich has come to a head ... Ipswich must have professional football'. It was signed 'J M Cobbold', John Dupuis' son and Chairman of Ipswich Town. Next week, all differences resolved, the two clubs were amalgamated, and Ipswich Town Football Club turned professional.

Football on Saturday afternoon, cinema in the evening. By 1937 there were six to choose from: Poole's Picture Palace in Tower Street, the Picture House in Tavern Street, the Central in Princes Street, the Regent at Major's Corner, the Ritz in Buttermarket, and the Odeon, just opened, in Lloyds Avenue. The first two had been in existence since 1910, Poole's having taken over the Lecture Hall of the Mechanics' Institute; after the second war it was converted into the Arts Theatre, the town's only one until its mantle was taken over by the Wolsey.

The Rev Thomas Jarrott's American Bioscope had introduced Ipswich to the new marvel at a lecture he gave in 1900 on the Boer War. This so impressed Arthur Churchman (the later tobacco baron) that in 1902 when he was Mayor, he commissioned Mr Jarrott to take some Animated Photographs of Edward VII's coronation procession. They were rushed back to Ipswich and shown to an audience of local worthies that evening in the Town Hall. The projector was set up at the back of the Sessions Court with a translucent screen placed in the doorway behind the Justices' seats leading to their retiring room. The doors were temporarily unhinged, and people sat either side of the screen, those in the retiring room viewing the pictures back to front. Afterwards, another huge screen was unfurled over the front door of the Town Hall itself, its gas floodlighting turned off, and the performance re-run for the crowd outside.

As the ploughshare had begun the rise of Ransomes in the nineteenth century, the combine harvester saw a quickening of its problems in the twentieth. The speed of the revolution wrought by this transatlantic monster after the Second World War took Ransomes and others by surprise, and much effort and money was expended trying to catch up with the Americans. At the same time the firm continued with an ambitious plan to move its multifarious activities to a vast 250-acre site at Nacton. One by one during the next forty years many of these operations, new and old, had to be closed down or sold, until in 1987 the decision was taken to concentrate on lawnmowers. By then much of the Nacton land, whose value rose as fast as its parent's fortunes sank, had been developed as a business park.

Its sister company, Ransome and Rapier, became a fatal casualty of that other, Thatcherite, revolution of the 1980's. Before his death in 1957, its managing director had been Dick Stokes, the town's Labour MP for twenty years; and the first of the series which, after the retirement in 1970 of Stokes' successor, Dingle Foot QC, has continued almost without interruption ever since.

Labour's social programme after the war added to the Council's financial responsibilities which were now ten times greater in real terms per head of the population than when Councillor Grimwade had complained a century earlier about his rates and taxes. Revenue expenditure reached £6m. in 1964, balanced by £2.4m. from the ratepayers, £1.5m. from charges for public services, and £2.1m from government grants. The shadow of central government and its money was beginning to overhang almost every aspect of the town's routine, an uneasy presence not felt except at intervals since the Norman tyranny of Roger Bigot.

Surveys were commissioned to enable the baleful eye of Whitehall to take a closer look at the amenities of Ipswich – its 'beautiful countryside', its port, its industrial infrastructure, its happy compact setting: surely these would provide an ideal environment for 70,000 of London's troublesome overspill? With natural growth it was reckoned they would increase the town's population from 117,000 to 250,000 by 1985. A linear new town to the east was considered, linking Ipswich and Felixstowe in a vast urban sprawl, but it was rejected in favour of development in the south and west where there was surplus sewage capacity and the prospect of what was called better integration. Housing, without garage space, was to be of high density, 60 people (20 houses) per acre, in order to encourage social contact and to save money on land purchase. Much post-war housing was said to be of poor quality: in future only the highest standards would be tolerated, an unsubstantiated and improbable assertion which nobody seems to have questioned. Nor was anything mentioned about the sort of Londoners who would live in them.

Local people were interviewed by sociologists, flattered by consultants and quizzed by pollsters. In one sample of 390, a majority, including all the Council, was in favour of the proposals, with 20 per cent against and as many undecided. Stick and carrot were employed, wrapped in jargon and wreathed in sinister and soothing clichés: 'painful necessity ... inevitability ... opportunity to do something different ... conserve what is good, improve what is not so good'. Ipswich would become 'a different kind of place' whose greater size would ease the solution of its many problems. City status was promised; the river, the 'shame of Ipswich', would be restored for recreation; the town centre from Christchurch Park to the Gipping would be pedestrianised; a by-pass bridge built over the Orwell; and victory gained perhaps by the enlarge community in both the Football League and the FA Cup, such as had been achieved by Liverpool in successive years after the planners had been busy there.

Priorities change, policies grow stale, and in 1969 the Minister decided against the scheme. During the years following, much of what had been promised was accomplished anyway: Ipswich had already triumphed in the Football League and soon did likewise in the FA Cup; the Orwell Bridge was built; the town centre was in part pedestrianised. Only the restoration of the Gipping's 'stinking ditch' and the dubious benefits of city status remained a mirage. Hopes for the latter are still entertained in some quarters – an application was composed in 1991 – but really the town is too small. The population in fact, having reached a peak in 1971 of 123,000, has been in gentle decline ever since, its first fall since the seventeenth century.

With hindsight, and considering similar experiments elsewhere, it may be said that the town had a lucky escape. It would indeed have been a different kind of place, transformed almost overnight by a handful of fallible experts and a pot of public money, not a convincing formula for success. Ipswich perforce would have adapted, and probably emerged into the twenty-first century after a traumatic generation still recognisable from the experience. There is a lot of ruin in an ancient town.

Bibliography

R J Aldous Ipswich 1826–47: The Politics of an English Borough (1979)
W G Arnott Orwell Estuary (1954)
E J Atkinson A School Remembered: Northgate Girls' School (1980)
H Austin Report on the Sanitary Conditions of Ipswich (1848)

N Bacon The Annals of Ipswich (1654)
G Ball Chantry Park and Mansion (1968)
A Ballard The Domesday Boroughs (1904)
C E Banks The Winthrop Fleet (1930)
C E Banks The Planters of the Commonwealth (1930)
J Blatchly The Town Library of Ipswich (1989)
J Blatchly 80 Ipswich Portraits (1980)
J E Bonney From Silent Street to Bolton Lane (1939)
J Browne A History of Congregationalism (1877)

R Canning Gifts and Legacies in the town of Ipswich (1819)
A Century of Service: The success story of the Ipswich Co-operative Society (1928)
P Clark Country towns in pre-industrial England (1981)
G R Clarke History of Ipswich (1830)
M Clegg Streets and Street Names in Ipswich (1984)
M Clegg The Way We Were (1989)
S Cobb 90 Years of Municipal Transport in Ipswich (1993)
R L Cross The Living Past (1975)
R L Cross Ipswich Markets and Fairs (1965)
R L Cross Justice in Ipswich (1968)

H C Darby The Domesday Geography of Eastern England (1952)
Diamond Jubilee of the Ipswich Industrial Co-operative Society (1928)
D Dymond and P Northeast A History of Suffolk (1985)

E Ekwall (ed) Oxford Dictionary of English Place Names (1960)
G E Evans Where Beards Wag All (1970)
N Evans The East Anglian Linen Industry (1985)
A Everitt Suffolk and the Great Rebellion, 1640–60 (1960)
H R Eyre The Drama and Theatre in Ipswich (1890)

R Finch A Cross in the Topsail (1979)
D Footman Dead Yesterday (1974)
G A Forecast Crown Street Story (1975)
A W Forsdike 150 Years of public service: a study of the gas industry in Ipswich (1977)
B Foster The Provision of Poor relief in Ipswich, 1800–44 (1977)

V Gibbs (ed) The Complete Peerage (1910)
J Glyde Moral, Social and Religious Conditions in Ipswich (1850)

J Glyde The New Suffolk Garland (1866)
J Glyde Materials for a History of Ipswich Races (1902)
J Glyde Materials for a Parliamentary History of Ipswich (1890)
J Glyde Notes for a Municipal History of Ipswich (1905)
R Gowing Public Men of Ipswich and East Suffolk (1875)
D Grace and D Phillips Ransomes of Ipswich (1975)
I Gray and W Potter Ipswich School, 1400–1950 (1950)
A J Green (ed) The Suffolk Martyrs (1851)

N Heard Wool: East Anglia's Golden Fleece (1970)
A P Hewett A Short History of St Nicholas' Old Meeting House (1959)
The History of Engineering in Ipswich (1949)
R Holder Aspects of Culture and Society in Elizabethan Ipswich (1984)
T J Hosken History of Congregationalism in Suffolk (1920)
W Hunt A Descriptive Handbook of Ipswich (1864)
J R Hutchinson The Administration of the Borough of Ipswich under Elizabeth I and James I (1952)

Ipswich Information, 1964–1973
Ipswich Labour Party Jubilee Year Book (1983)

R Jenkins Industries in Suffolk (1939)
H M Jewell English Local Administration in the Middle Ages (1972)
A G E Jones Shipbuilding in Ipswich (1957)
D L Jones The Story of Swimming in Ipswich (1985)
T Jones Ipswich Inns, Taverns and Pubs (1991)
Jubilee of the Ipswich and Suffolk Freehold Land Society (1899)

Kelly's Directories for Ipswich and Suffolk
D Knowles and R Hadcock Medieval Religious Houses, England and Wales (1953)

N Layard 17 Suffolk Martyrs (1902)
J Leather The Shipbuilding Bayleys (1965)
H R Lingwood Ipswich Playhouses (1936)

R Malster Ipswich: Town on the Orwell (1978)
R Malster and R Jones A Victorian Vision (1992)
R Markham A Rhino in the High Street (1990)
R Markham Public Transport in Ipswich (1971)
A Moffat Air Raids on Ipswich (1946)
H Moffat East Anglian's First Railways (1987)
G Moore Smith and P Reaney The Family of Withypool (1936)
K O Morgan (ed) Oxford History of Britain (1988)
D P Mortlock Popular Guide to Suffolk Churches (1990)
H Munro Cautley Suffolk Churches (1982)

The Official Guide to Ipswich (1948)
A Owen The Presbyterian Interest in Ipswich (1967)

W Page (ed) Victoria History of the County of Suffolk (1911)
N Pevsner The Buildings of England: Suffolk (1961)
E Powell The Rising in East Anglia (1896)
E Powell (ed) A Suffolk Hundred in the year 1283 (1910)
C M Prescott Suffolk Constabulary in the 19th Century (1967)
K Price History of Ipswich Town Football Club (1973)
Proceedings of the Suffolk Institute of Archaeology

R Ratcliff History of the Working Class Movement in Ipswich (1953)
M Read Ipswich in the 17th Century (1973)
M Read Ipswich probate Inventories 1583–1631 (1981)
P Reaney The Origin of English Place Names (1960)
L Redstone Ipswich through the ages (1948)
V B Redstone The Ancient House (1912)
V B Redstone Summaries from the Extract of Ipswich Borough Records (1926)
V B Redstone The Dutch and Huguenot Settlements in Ipswich (1921)
Report of the Committee on the Poor and the Workhouse, Ipswich (1819)
T N Ritson (ed) The History of Wesleyan Methodism (1908)
A Rumble (ed) Domesday Book: Suffolk (1986)

J C Sadler A History of the Ipswich Mint (1975)
R K Sergeant A History of the Ipswich Ragged School, 1849–79 (1979)
The Shankland-Cox Report on Ipswich Expansion (1966)
W W Skeat The Place Names of Suffolk (1913)
S Smith The Madonna of Ipswich (1980)
S Smith The Apostle to Ipswich: L' Abbé Louis-Pierre Simon (1978)
Souvenir of the TUC at Ipswich (1909)
G T Speke Corporation of Ipswich and the Education Provisions (1980)
F M Stenton Anglo-Saxon England (1971)
J M Stratton Agricultural Records 220–1968 (1969)
Struggle: A short history of Ipswich and District Trades Council, 1885–1967 (1969)
Suffolk Leaders: Social and Political (1906)
The Suffolk Review

J H Thomson A guide to St Pancras Church (1961)
L P Thompson Tales of Old Ipswich (1938)

Union Workhouse: Guardians' Minutes and Accounts
Union Workhouse: Relieving Officers' Reports
H R Unwin A History of Tacket St Congregational Church in Ipswich (1977)

K Wade Origins of Ipswich (1981)
H E Walton Notes on Workhouses in Suffolk (1965)
E Ward and others 350 Years of Ipswich (USA) History (1984)
W D Warren A Century of Witness and Service (1960)
C and M Weaver Ransomes, 1789–1989 (1989)
J Webb Poor Relief in Elizabethan Ipswich (1966)
J Webb Great Tooley of Ipswich (1962)
R Webber The Peasants' Revolt (1980)
R Welldon Finn Domesday Book: a guide (1973)
R Welldon Finn Domesday Studies: the Eastern Counties (1967)
P A Welsby Churches and People in Victorian Ipswich (1963)
W Westrip and S Bonner A Century of Service: St Matthew's School (1947)
E White The Old Inns and Taverns of Ipswich (1885)
G Williamson The Ingenious Mr Gainsborough (1972)
J Wodderspoon Memorials of the ancient town of Ipswich (1850)
F Woolnough Short History of the Mansion and Estate of Christchurch (1913)

INDEX

of Suffolk names and places